Best wishes
at home & work

# YOU CAN'T FIRE ME

# I'M YOUR FATHER

# YOU CAN'T CAN'T FIRE ME I'M YOUR FATHER

## WHAT EVERY FAMILY BUSINESS SHOULD KNOW

## Neil N. Koenig, Ph.D.

HILLSBORO PRESS

FRANKLIN, TENNESSEE

Printed in the United States of America

03    02    01    00    99            1    2    3    4    5

Library of Congress Catalog Card Number: 98-75322

ISBN: 1-57736-120-2

*Cover design by Gary Bozeman*

Published by
HILLSBORO PRESS
An imprint of
PROVIDENCE HOUSE PUBLISHERS
238 Seaboard Lane • Franklin, Tennessee 37067
800-321-5692
www.providencehouse.com

### For my parents

who taught me, by the way
they live, the values that stand
the test of time

### For Forrest

who called one morning out of
the blue and said, "Dad, write a book.
Cortney and I would like a record
of what you've been thinking about
at work all these years."

### For Cortney

whose fine mind and big heart
make her an uncommon young
woman

# CONTENTS

# PREFACE

Although theory has its place, real people are so much more interesting. And instructive. I have learned more about family business from actual families in business than I could possibly have learned from any other source.

The content of this book is thus driven by my experiences over the past thirty years working with families, work that has involved countless hours of listening to families and learning from them what is important. Each chapter deals with issues I have seen families grapple with as they strive to make something meaningful at their work and in their homes. Fortunately, there is enough that is common among families everywhere to make generalizations. Otherwise, we could not learn from each other.

I have attempted to be faithful to the people who have invited me into their lives. I want to give voice to family members in family business. Hence, the quotations, stories, and profiles in each chapter. In all cases, they are genuine. I have of course changed their names and any possible identifying information in order to protect their privacy and to maintain the professional confidentiality they deserve.

It is my hope that readers will benefit from others' experiences and issues as I have.

# ACKNOWLEDGMENTS

This effort would not have been possible without the encouragement of the following good people. To each I owe my best thanks.

Leon Dermenjian, owner of a truly world-class family business

Bill Nicholson, who has shown me the past twenty-five years what good can be done in the world of business

Jerry Cook, who invited me into the world of business in the first place

Alan Pierrot, MD, chairman of my board

Brent Stolpestad, for the mental health breaks

Bud Richter, for encouragement in the early going of this book

Rollie Wussow, for the first green light for this book

Stephen James, for patiently walking me through the world of publishing

Kyle Stephenson and Rudy Neufeld, for the family business forums

Bill and Art Phillips, my first family business clients

The many family businesses who have done me the favor of providing meaningful work.

# INTRODUCTION

Family businesses do not enjoy a wonderful reputation, in spite of all the good they do and their huge presence across the world's economy.

Talk with insiders and they tell you a family business is no picnic. You end up wondering why they even bother to stay in business together. Before too long in a conversation, fathers grit their teeth and snarl, "You can't tell kids anything these days. They've got a mind of their own." Mothers worry that the business will cause their children to not love each other as much as she loves each and every one of them. Brothers and sisters have unspoken performance and attitude evaluations of each other that are anything but high praise. Many children even "fire" their parents along the way.

Parents get fired on and off during the course of family business. Children claim their parents do not listen, are not open to new ideas, preach too much, have to have things their own way too often, act like they know it all because of all their experience, play perceived favorites, want to be too helpful and protective, and want to operate the business as though it were still in its infancy when the entrepreneur approach was so successful. The list goes on and on. Fortunately, children rehire their parents before too long. Until the next episode. But love works that way.

Naturally parents sometimes also feel like "firing" their kids. They get frustrated with the work ethic of the new generation, the open and often blunt communication styles of young people, the faith the younger generation has in education and computers, the entitlement mentality some have, the casualness around money and relationships, the sibling rivalry, the seeming allergy the young have to well-meaning advice and help, and the confidence bordering on cockiness many children have when they picture themselves running things their way. Fortunately, parents almost never ever fire their children, no matter how much they would like to. Love works that way.

Talk to outsiders familiar with family businesses and you come away wondering why they even work for a family business in the first place. Accountants, attorneys, and consultants quickly roll their eyes when the topic is family business. My own accountant recently told me, "The worst businesses there are are family businesses. They just can't get past all their family stuff. They won't benefit from any book."

In family businesses, many nonfamily employees, especially those in management, have their lists of complaints about how the family's "crappy stuff" affects everyday work. What they find most galling is the all too typical monopoly the family exercises on thinking, planning, and decision making.

And then there is family business literature. There is seldom an article or book written that does not solemnly lament the hard facts. Family businesses, while comprising almost half of the world's economy, with over eight million in the United States alone, face some pretty tough odds. Seven of ten family businesses do not survive into the second generation; two of the remaining three do not survive into the third generation; and the typical family business has a life expectancy of only twenty-four years.[1] And there are many old sayings reflecting these daunting facts: "Grandfather merchant, son playboy, grandson beggar"; "From shirtsleeves to shirtsleeves in three generations"; "From sandals to sandals in three generations." Magazine articles in particular dwell on stories about family feuds, litigation, the founder's "trap," Cain and Abel redux, bankruptcy, and so on.

It is as though family businesses are one big hopeless mess. This, of course, is not fair. There are many thousands, if not millions, of successful families in business together and loving it, not every minute, but loving it nonetheless. They love the experience of working with people they care most about, creating with them something of worth, for themselves, for their children and grandchildren, for their employees, for their customers, and for their communities. They are proud of their dream, their hard work, their sacrifices, the risks they took, the results they have achieved, and the good standing they enjoy in their communities and industries.

How these successful families approach their personal and work lives comprises a body of best practices that can be emulated by other families in business together. These best practices can be implemented by families in the early going, during critical but normal stages of growth, at crisis points, or even when it seems too late—it is never too late when family members earnestly want things to be better.

This book is about best practices in family business gleaned from my thirty years of working with families. It is especially about the best practices concerning family matters. It is the family matters that distinguish family businesses from all others. It can be said that family businesses are no different than other businesses when it comes to doing business. They too must meet the dictates of the customer, have enlightened leadership, implement effective management and systems, use technology wisely, manage money smartly, play in the dizzying global economy, and have intelligent ownership and management succession plans. Family businesses, however, have an added, inescapable, and most compelling other dimension—family matters. It is family matters that can make or break a family enterprise, regardless of how skillfully the strictly business side is done.

It is the family stuff that brings out the deepest satisfaction, and the deepest worry. The strongest commitments, and the most fragile feelings. The most selfless generosity, and the most petty selfishness. The greatest sense of belonging, and the longest distance of alienation. The finest acts of forgiveness, and the worst acts of revenge. The best examples of merit, and the worst examples of entitlement. The most energizing of dreams, and the most heartbreaking disappointments.

As if business alone were not challenging enough, family business, because of family matters, is even more challenging. It is not for the faint of heart. Families in business together are people who are either brave enough, or foolish enough, to try and do what most people shy away from. They try to run successful businesses while they attempt to run successful families, all the while working with each other day in and day out! And on top of this, they try to make and carry out smart ownership decisions to ensure not only their standards of living, and those of their children and their children's children, but also those of their employees and the economy of their communities.

Family business is for people I admire. People who . . .

• Believe in family life: families are to die for

• Believe in work as part of personal and spiritual fulfillment

• Believe in business as a way to express dreams and talents, and as a means to do good

• Believe their family business can be the best of two worlds—love and work, both at the same time

# PART ONE

# The Family's Business

# CHAPTER ONE
# It's a Matter of Priorities and Boundaries

*What matters most to us? I'd have to say our family's business. Our family relationships have taken a beating over the years as everything was sacrificed for the sake of the business. Like I say, we're not much of a family.*

Elton, age seventy-one

*What matters most to us? No question about it. It's our family. I suppose we'd be more successful some other way, but goodness, the family comes first. We don't want to be like other businesses. Our business is family.*

Helen, age seventy-three

*What matters most to us? The way things have been these past several years, I'd have to say nothing. Dad isn't tending to the business anymore. He just got sick of it after years of 100-hour work weeks. And our family is nothing. No one is close to each other. And this remarriage stuff, with artificial brothers and sisters, just hasn't panned out. I'm sick of the whole thing.*

Todd, age thirty-one

*What matters most to us? We're trying like heck to have a good family life. But we're all dedicated to making our business a success too. It's not easy. Sometimes it's like trying to juggle two bowling balls. But it's worth it. For us it's really a no-brainer—we're not going to ruin home life for the sake of getting rich, and we're not going to blow our business. So we're trying to do both.*

Mike, age thirty-six

ASK ANY FAMILY MEMBER OF A FAMILY BUSINESS WHAT the family's top priorities are and the first answer likely will be "our family and our business." Good answer. But many family members upon further reflection will admit something else. The history of too many family businesses suggests something else as well.

## THE BUSINESS/FAMILY PRIORITY DIAGRAM

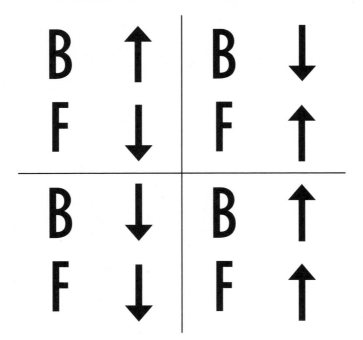

Too many family business people live as though what matters most to them has to be either the business or the family—either/or, or neither. Some families have placed top priority on the business, to the neglect of the family. Some have placed top priority on the family, to the neglect of the business. Some have chosen the worst of all worlds, placing no priority on either the family or the business. These families over the long haul contribute significantly to the poor reputation family businesses have in conversation and in print.

There are successful families in business together, however, that practice two priorities at the same time. They struggle mightily to give both their families and businesses the highest of priorities, both equally. These families have a lifelong commitment to thrive as families and run thriving businesses. Their approach is the most important family business best practice there is. They give top billing in their daily lives to both home and work at the same time.

The above graphic illustrates the four priority choices from which every family business can choose. The arrows represent priority: pointing up means top priority, pointing down means low priority.

## BUSINESS AS TOP PRIORITY

**B ↑**
**F ↓**

One group of family business owners operates on a day in, day out basis as though their business matters more than anything else in life. The business dominates every-thing. It consumes them. This is especially true for first generation founders. Starting a business requires enormous time and energy. And the rewards are seductive. The business, although a real task master, is exciting, engrossing, captivating, and risky—great rewards all. And the early successes beget even more effort and rewards. The sacri-fice required, which takes no prisoners, is exhausting, but does not feel exhausting. The founder is doing what he loves. He is working with his heart as well as his head as he pours every waking hour, and every sleepless night, into the business.

Trouble is, the family takes a real hit, especially a young marriage and young children. This is common for many founders who start working on their dream early in adulthood. Over a period of time, patterns set in that only later are revealed as hard on the family.

All family conversation is about nothing except the business. It dominates table talk if the founder gets home early enough to eat with the family. It is the topic of choice at birthday parties for the children, on holidays, on vacations, and on phone calls practically every evening. Eventually someone, usually a young adult or a spouse, cries out, "Why can't we talk about something other than the darn business? I'm sick of the business! Don't we know that there's other things in life?" Families that place top priority on the business can end up not knowing what else life has to offer.

Marriages of course suffer from neglect. Two well-meaning persons, well matched, sharing similar values and dreams, end up strangers to each other.

> *I was married to the children and my husband was married to his business. Now we are not friends at all. We are occasional lovers, occasional enemies, but mostly occasional roommates. And when Elton finally really retires, if he ever does, I'll be darned if he's going to sit around here and expect me to wait on him hand and foot like they have done for him at the office all these years. I'll shoo him out of here. They can keep taking care of him at the office, or he can play golf and cards all day, every day, at the club.*
>
> Edna, age sixty-nine, married to
> Elton, semiretired founder,
> agricultural chemical company

Relationships to children are neglected. Even though the founder may truly love his children, and feel deep down that he is doing it all for his kids—"I want my kids to have it better than I had it"—the founder ends up a stranger to his children and they to him.

*I really don't know my dad. At least not like other people know him. I stand in awe of him when I watch him talking to other people. He really knows a lot, and is an interesting guy. When he's at work he's amazing. But when he's home he's like nothing. You just know his mind is on work. And rather than admit he loves it, he crabs about work. Always complaining and worrying he's going to lose it all. And when he does talk to us it's like a performance review. I wish I could get to know my dad the way others know him, as a real guy.*

Matt, age twenty-one, student

The highest price families pay for overprioritizing the business comes from the tendency to use the business as the measurement of family members' worth. Children are either accidentally or deliberately valued, based on their fit for the business. Somehow the children are scripted to fit into the business, which is very different than being scripted to fit into the family. The child with a nose for business, with talents that are needed at work, with the drive and ambition of the "old man" is prized. The child who walks to the beat of a different drummer, who is gifted in other areas, for example, the arts, or who has little interest in business, much less the family's particular business, or who is unsure of what he or she wants to become, is the child who ends up feeling outside the family. When old enough to articulate complex feelings, they lament, "I've not felt valued, or prized, let alone wanted. I'll be damned if I'll ever sing for my father."

When founders, or succeeding generation family business leaders who work all the time, are finally insightful enough to articulate complex feelings about what they have done, they inevitably lament:

*If I had it to do over again, I would've spent more time with the family. I poured everything into the business. It was go, go, go all the time when I was getting things started. And when we started to get a little bit ahead, I couldn't let go. The business needed me. It's been my whole life. But I can see now that my family needed me too. My wife, Edna, raised the kids alone. They really didn't get to*

*know me, and when I was around, I was way too damn hard on*
*them. I know I drove my oldest boy away. I couldn't see that he just*
*wasn't cut out for a business life. So we never got along. He's a mess*
*now, divorced and all. Feels like a black sheep. My daughter's in*
*the business, thank God. But she's just like me—a real hard driver.*
*I wonder if her husband will put up with her the way Edna put up*
*with me. I know her kids miss her. And as far as Edna and me go,*
*I guess she has always felt left out. The two of us don't do much*
*together. Never did, once the kids came along and I got started. I*
*don't know, I guess we just always put the business first. It's all I*
*know. Sure, we're well off, but we're not much of a family.*

> Elton, age seventy-one, semiretired
> founder, agricultural
> chemical company

## FAMILY AS TOP PRIORITY

**B ↓**
**F ↑**

A second group of family business owners takes the family approach to business. Their businesses mean family. Running the business like a business is not on the agenda. They are not very interested in the outside business world, let alone the organizational revolution of the past two decades. What exemplary companies outside and within their own industries do does not especially concern these families. Their businesses, instead, are run like family—emotionally, impulsively, and protectively.

It is common to find family, family, family all over the place in these companies. Family is hired because of who they are, not because of what they can do, what they know, what education and training they have, or what experience they can bring to the business. Leadership is determined by birthright, birth order, and personality, unless the family pays allegiance to the divine right of the oldest son—then personality does not even count. Children are often not required to achieve much education and training that is germane to the family business. Their preparation for work is an apprenticeship within the company from midteen years on, no outside experience needed. Family is rewarded for who they are, not for what they accomplish.

Employees are just that—employees—usually regarded as extensions of the family, again regardless of their performance, or as cost factors that do not need benefits such as pensions or retirement plans. Nonfamily employees seldom are in the inner circle of thinking, planning, and decision making. They definitely are not privy to the financial scores of the business. Usually the family is embarrassed by the large amount of money the company deals with (as though outsiders do not figure things out anyway, although they usually have an exaggerated guess). Occasionally some families are embarrassed by how little money is involved, hoping employees and community people do not see them as "all hat and no cattle," as the old Texas saying goes.

These families are content to do what has gotten them this far: hard work, some loyal customers, a good local name, and family loyalty to the business. They have a hard time believing that they may be the next mom and pop outfit to get run over by some mercilessly efficient, ruthlessly aggressive national or international company that will win over their loyal customers with quality, speed, price, and convenience.

They will blame the times, or El Niño, or government red tape when they get run over. But they will have a hard time seeing that overprioritizing their own family, as wonderful as family is, played a big role in their inability to respond to a changing marketplace with a talented, flexible, and smart organization.

*We're doing this for the family. We don't let business interfere with our relationships, like other businesses do. Those businesses could care less about their people. Loyalty doesn't exist out there anymore. That's why we work for ourselves. We make a nice living by providing jobs for all of us. We not only believe in nepotism, I guess that's the word for it, but we practice it. Even for shirttail relatives. We have family members in all key positions. Who else can we trust? We probably could be more successful, but at what price? We're content to go along as we have been, taking care of our own. The good Lord willing, our grandchildren can work here someday. We just want to take care of our own.*

Helen, age seventy-three, mother,
cofounder/bookkeeper,
retail appliance store

## NEITHER ONE AS TOP PRIORITY

**B** ↓
**F** ↓

This is the worst of all approaches to family business. Neither the family nor the business is emphasized. One or the other is in shambles, with the other on the verge of becoming so. This is seldom seen in the early going, when young enthusiasm fuels the entrepreneur, regardless of his or her age. More likely, this no-priorities-for-anything-we're-about comes late in the first generation and famously during the second generation.

In the first generation, it is the worn-out founder who can end up without any vital or vigorous priorities. After decades of hard work he finds himself sick of it—the hours, the worries, the headaches, the relentless competition, the changing workforce, the paperwork, the computers, the red tape. Because he did it all at work, he has no one ready and qualified to succeed him. Because he is slowing down, his business struggles with only part-time, semiretired leadership and lackluster management. For the first time in his life he feels no get-up-and-go for work.

He never took the time to develop any sort of life outside of work. He finds nothing fulfilling or satisfying at home or at leisure. His children are strangers to him, and he to them. His wife is now a stranger to him, and he to her. His influence in business and civic circles is steadily diminishing, partly because of his age and his exhaustion, and partly because everyone can see that the very thing that has defined this gentleman is now eroding. For his long years of hard work, all he has to show is a big, empty house. His family life long ago went to hell, and now the business follows.

This worst of all approaches, neither the family nor the business receiving top priority, can also occur during the second generation. This is where the playboy of "Grandfather merchant, son playboy, grandson beggar" comes in. Typically, everything is handed to him on a silver platter. Usually he advances in title and perquisites until becoming president and CEO—not because he is qualified, but because his family practices the "divine right of the firstborn male." When he does work, he parachutes in and takes a command and control approach, as though he were on top of things on a daily basis. Although they enjoy him, basically nonfamily employees do not respect him. He works when he feels like it, allowing as much time as possible for his hobbies and his complicated family life.

Extended family life for this playboy is almost always boring, unless there is a huge argument, something for which he has real talent. He can turn on the charm and say all the right things with his grandmother and aunts. But he has disdain for the pedestrian tastes and lifestyles of the rest of the extended family. He is usually patronizing to his siblings, kindly in a way, but never emotionally close, always going through the motions with them, but never really committed to them, or interested in their development in the family's company.

The personal family life of the second generation playboy is often a series of broken impulses. The first wife was married when each was too young, but "they had to get married." The second wife was a trophy, but a classic gold digger on whom he lavished travel and jewelry. She never connected with his children from the first marriage, but then wife number one would not allow her to anyway. Wife number three was a strong professional, liberated woman who found him gallant, sexy, and shallow. His insecurities do not permit a competent woman to have an independent, parallel life, so his smothering approach drove the new-age woman away too. Meantime he bought expensive gifts for his children, and never said no to them, in hopes of their devotion. In a serious interview about his life in family business he says with a devilish grin, "You know, I spent 90 percent of my time and money on wine and women, and the other 10 percent I wasted."

## WE DON'T AGREE ON WHAT COMES FIRST

**B ? F**

There is a large group of family business people who do not agree amongst each other about what should receive the highest priority, their families or their business. They are not on the same page with one another. What comes first varies from family member to family member, and from time to time.

Many families do not agree simply because of individual differences. Spouses have different priorities, needs, wants, and expectations. Children are their own persons, to be sure, who may or may not give a rip about business, let alone the family's business. Families with members from the Depression generation, the boomer generation, and generation X will have big differences of approach to work, love, leisure, health, money, and religion. Then too, some family members value only the short term, and will press for immediate returns, returns the long termers wish to delay. And families in an early developmental stage, like those with infants or young school-age children, will have different priorities than the retirement-age founder whose only passions are business and golf.

The absence of carefully agreed upon decisions about what matters most to all family members is glaringly exposed when things are stressful at home. When the demands of work, especially during the start-up phase or during a business downturn, require industrial strength amounts of time, energy, worry, and money, home life gets short shrift. And when home life is neglected too long, problems inevitably develop. The business gets blamed. So, in order for the family members to address personal matters, the business temporarily is neglected. Once home is restored to normal the business is back to being priority number one. Now home life is blamed for the added difficulties that have been accumulating back at the shop. Caught in such stressful situations, families often exclaim, "We don't agree on what comes first."

> *Ever since my husband took over the business after his dad died, he has been killing himself trying to prove he can make it on his own. I'm worried about him, but also worried about us. He hasn't tucked the kids into bed for months. Our oldest fights sleep, waiting for his daddy. And he wants him to come to his first T-ball game. Deep in his little heart he's worried Jack won't make it. As for our marriage . . . What marriage? I feel like I'm a widow, just like his mom is now. She put up with this type of life thirty years ago. But I won't! Family should matter most. Not the business. I'd rather be poorer, with a husband that is home nights and weekends. But if I breathe a word about selling the business, Jack goes ballistic. He needs to succeed as much as I want a decent family life. We're really in a crisis.*
>
> Jennifer, age thirty-four, homemaker, wife of
> part owner of an agri-products hauling firm

## BUSINESS AND FAMILY: BOTH TOP PRIORITIES

**B ↑**

**F ↑**

There are families in business together who are taking the "the road less traveled." They earnestly want both a successful family life and a successful business. They are all on the same page, valiantly working at living a balanced lifestyle. These families are unsung heroes. They resist the easy temptations of an imbalanced lifestyle, choosing instead to live what they truly value—each other and their work. They are families that mean family, and families that mean business. It is as though they advised Sigmund Freud a century ago when he claimed that the essence of life is to love and to work. Both.

*I have real good, close relationships at home. And our business is doing fine too. Sure, we have bumps along the way, both at home and at work. And yes, sometimes I get things out of balance. Some times of the year are busier than others, especially late summer and fall during harvest. But my family understands. They know I miss them. But I'm sure we all know that when things slow down, we'll be tight again. And at work they all know I'm not going to work seven days a week year round. I've let them all know that my family comes first most of the time. And I make sure everyone else at work has the chance to be good family people too. What would I have if I lost my family or my business? Or both? To me, I want both, just like I want my cake and eat it too. Why not?*

Jeff, age thirty-eight, second generation
head of a diversified family farm

These families do not have an easy time of it. Were it not for the satisfaction of living up to their values, and for the long-term benefits of living a balanced lifestyle, these families would cave into easier temptations. They diligently run their business like a business. They carry out the purpose of their business and operate according to their company values. They meet the needs of their customers with quality, speed, cost, and convenience. They develop a management team that is informed and skilled and capable of bringing out the best in the company's employees. They hire well, hiring people who fit into their company's culture, training them for higher levels of performance. They know where they are going as a company—they have direction, and know at least generally how to get there (a strategic plan). They make good use of technology and money, and they reward themselves and their employee partners when results permit.

All the while these families are running their businesses like businesses, they place top priority on their families. They do this by making time for family. They know families need time, just like a baby needs holding and a start-up company needs capital. Families require time. Love does not grow on trees, no more than money does.

These families are couples who take the time to still go out on dates with each other. They talk with each other daily. These families are parents who take the time from work so they can participate with their children in the classroom and on the sporting fields. These parents take the time to play with their young children, read to them and with them, and have quality "good nights" with them. These parents take the time to listen to their teenagers, set tough limits on behavior, and enjoy teenage goofiness.

These families are extended families that take the time to help each other out when needed. They enjoy each other's company on occasion, but are not so close as extended family to violate the sanctity of private relationships. These families, in other words, have a commitment to each other, and live out that commitment, without smothering each other.

Obviously there has never been a family that has ever been able to pull off this dual priority approach to family business perfectly. Difficulties, problems, growth pains, and conflicts are normal and inevitable. And obviously these families accept the reality that no one can have it all totally. "Totally" is the operative word here. These families' businesses would most likely be bigger, richer, more efficient, more whatever, were the family members to give the business every ounce of their energy and every moment of their time. But they refuse to cheat their families. They end up having to sacrifice here and there at work in order to have a home life.

Families that want both a good home life and work life realize that their family life would be closer, more relaxed, more fun, easier, more whatever, were they to give less time to work and more time to each other. But they refuse to cheat their family's business. They end up having to sacrifice here and there at home in order to advance the business.

These families willingly practice disciplined trade-offs to "have it all," knowing full well that "having it all" means never settling for one without the other.

*It's really tough keeping it all in balance. I could be at the office twenty-four hours a day every day of the week, and still not get done what I want. And you know, I love it. I love my work. We've got opportunities all over the place. But some are going to have to wait. Can't do it all, because I want a home life too. I've got a wonderful wife—she's my best friend. And our two kids are really something. My favorite time of the day is when I get home. I make it a practice to leave the office no later than 6:00 P.M. (sometimes I end up working at home later in the evening). The girls are looking for me out the window in front of the house. I actually call ahead from the car to let them know I'm coming. My wife works too, but not at our family business—we need and want separate lives. There's dinner, getting the kids ready for bed, and picking up the place. By the time we finally have time for each other alone, we're pooped. But we force ourselves to at least talk, with some music on, for a half hour or so several nights a week. And we go out on dates every other weekend. It's all worth it, but it's not easy. It'd be easier to cave in and do just one thing. What worries me is how it wouldn't take much to upset our balancing act. If something bad happened, something would have to give. But I believe we could handle it.*

Mike, age thirty-six, founder's son,
president/CEO, construction company

## BOUNDARIES

The road less taken—family business people placing top priority on both work and love—is immeasurably easier to travel when families observe another family business best practice. It is the practice of boundaries. The most successful families respect two critically valuable boundaries. One is the boundary between the family and the business, the other the boundary between ownership and management.

### The Family/Business Boundary

The family/business boundary is a day-in and day-out necessity. It is about preventing interference between the two worlds in which family business people live.

Many families understand the importance of professional behavior at work. An example of this boundary is how so many children at work call their parents by their first names. It is embarrassing to use "mom" or "dad" when talking, for example, with deal makers over a business opportunity. This boundary prevents family junk like bad moods, raw feelings, and arguments at home from tres-

# Family Life ⋮ Business Life

passing onto the business field. It outlaws any negative talk to people at work about family members behind their backs. Any divulging of personal, confidential information about family is prevented. Any blatant use of company funds for personal matters is prohibited. Family sacred cows are not allowed: family members working in the company are treated as nonfamily, with no more and no less privilege, opportunity, stress, reward, and accountability than anyone else.

The family/business boundary also works wonders at home. The junk of the business does not come home. Business is not the only topic of interest. Business is not used as the yardstick to measure family relationships and individual beauty. Business does not rob the family of having a life. An example of this boundary in action is the practice of setting aside one day a week, like Sunday, when "thou shalt not work" is augmented with "thou shalt make Sundays a 100 percent family day."

When the important boundary between family life and business life is respected, families live and work with the discipline to keep them as separate as possible. Business is business, family is family. There is a time and place for each. Boundaries merely reinforce what everyone knows anyway: people know where to talk about what, when to talk about what, and whom to talk to about what. This is a matter of common sense, appropriateness, manners, discretion, and priorities. Boundaries assist families in maximizing their commitment to each of their top priorities—home life and work life.

It is important to recognize that a boundary is not a tall, brick wall. It is a dotted line of permeability. It is nonsense to think that the family does not or should not lend strength to the business. Or that the business should not lend much to the family. On the contrary. The beauty of family business is the experience of working with loved ones who are doing what they love to do. The cross benefits of their two worlds are enviable rewards in themselves.

### Ownership/Management Boundary

The second boundary important to families who place the highest priority on both family and business is the boundary between ownership and management. This boundary is the first and most critical ownership issue families need to work out during family meetings (see chapter 13).

The ownership/management boundary is about sharp distinctions. Ownership is about love; management is about talent and skill. Ownership is about who you are; management is about what you can do. Ownership is your last name; management is performance. Ownership is given; management is earned. Ownership is family membership; management is education, training, and experience. Ownership is about doing the right things; management is about doing things right.[1] Ownership is about the big picture for

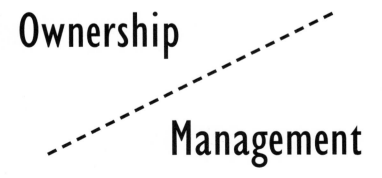

succeeding generations; management is about Monday through Friday implementation of the big picture.

This boundary recognizes that simply because someone owns something does not mean he has to run it, should run it, or even has to know how to run it. This is particularly true of third and later generations owning family businesses. At this stage of the corporate life cycle, it is common to have most of management, if not also senior executive leadership, in the hands of nonfamily professionals. By this time it is crucial to have a professional board of directors with crucial seats reserved for outsiders. The family meets as an ownership board, dealing with ownership issues, leaving management issues to the board of directors and to management, holding each accountable to the family owners.

Many families chafe at the influence of outsiders in management. For them it is a matter of pride—they do not want outsiders to know insider stuff. But more powerfully, it is a huge trust factor: "Who else can you trust? That's why we have family in all key positions." I have often challenged this fear by asking if, given the choice between a brother-in-law who is a bookkeeper and an outsider CPA experienced in estate planning and financial planning, whom the family would pick to assure their grandchildren's financial futures. Or would the family choose their dental- hygienist daughter over an orthodontist for their grandchildren's needed dental corrections?

If family members have the skill, education, training, and personalities for management, all the better. But if family does not have what it takes to run a complex, challenging organization in this rugged economy—an organization that is being counted on for the next generations' benefit—then the family has the responsibility to observe the ownership/management boundary by hiring good qualified professionals who can be trusted to competently run the business.

## SUMMARY

The joys and rewards of working with family to make something of worth are missed by family business people who either put work first, at the expense of love, or put love first, at the expense of successful work, or put neither first, or disagree about what to put first.

The most successful family business people implement two best practices. First, they place equally powerful priority on both their family lives and their business lives, so that they can work with loved ones doing what they love to do. They accept the almost daily discipline this requires and the tradeoffs that go with it. Secondly, they use boundaries to keep work from overwhelming home, and home from subtracting from work. They also use boundaries to keep ownership and management as distinct roles and responsibilities. When they consider all other options and temptations, these families stick to their priorities and boundaries.

## BACK TO THE BASICS

1. Discuss with family members where your family is on the "Business/Family Priority Diagram."
2. List five ways you have successfully kept your business from overwhelming your family life.
3. List five ways you have successfully kept your family life from subtracting from your business success.
4. Ask family members what they think your top five priorities are, both at work and at home.
5. Over the past six months, how have you spent your evenings and weekends? Do your findings please you and your family?

## CHAPTER TWO

# Let's Run This Outfit Like a Business

*The biggest frustration for me, and I'm a family member, is how we don't run our business like a business. I had no intention of joining our family business. I went off to college, worked out of state for four years, and got my M.B.A. But then Dad's health started failing him. He called me to come home and run the business. My sister and two brothers, who have been with the company right out of high school, had a fit. They have no intention of working any differently than before. Our employees are very willing to make the necessary changes. But not my own family members. They're in it just for themselves, expecting the business to just take care of them. They're my biggest challenge. The rest of the business is easy.*

Tom, age thirty-three,
president/CEO, insurance agency

PETER DRUCKER, THE MOST INFLUENTIAL THINKER about business and management this past half century, makes it crystal clear that the business of a family business is business. Period. "The family serves the business. Neither will do well if the business is run to serve the family. The controlling word in 'family business' is not 'family.' It has to be 'business.'"[1] The wisdom here comes from the countless family businesses that have been ruined because the families treated their businesses not as a responsibility, but as a privilege.

It is easy to understand how family business owners can succumb to the temptation of running their businesses as a source of privilege. After all, they are owners. And in our society ownership equates with license—you can do anything you darn please, as long as you own it. With ownership comes power, final decision-making authority, control of information, and of course, rewards. It is only one small step, then, to fall for a host of privileges that are perceived by family members as rightly coming to them.

## PRIVILEGES

There is the financial privilege. Some family businesses operate as though the spoils of business come with the family name. Ignoring the need to be profitable, to make capital improvements, to set aside capital reserves, to pay down debt, or to pay competitive wages to nonfamily employees, these families milk their businesses for every cent they can. "Legitimate" business expenses include providing all family members and spouses with cars, gas credit cards, auto insurance, auto maintenance and repairs, and even car washes and detailing. Family members are provided free cellular phones, home computers, all insurance coverage, home repair, maid and gardening services, postage, and even toilet paper dragged home from the office. All accounting and legal services are family perks. So is the vacation home, and the year- end bonuses for Christmas shopping. Virtually anything that can be gotten away with, for the sake of family membership, is tried, regardless of the financial needs of the business.

There is also the position privilege. Setting aside business sense and common sense, some family businesses reserve all executive positions for family members only, regardless of aptitude, education, training, experience, skills, or results of prior performance.

A retiring founder of a $32 million sales-per-year manufacturing company placed his only son (daughters weren't even considered) in the president/chief executive officer chair. The thirty-three-year-old young man had not gone past high school, never read a business book, and had only sporadically worked in the company at menial jobs as a teenager. But he needed a job. And father, for sentimental reasons, wanted the company to be in family hands at the top. Key employees were to babysit their new executive during his OJT (on-the-job-training), while having to endure the son's anemic, although aggressive, imitations of his father's entrepreneurial style of leadership. They knew the organization was well beyond its start-up stage, requiring a different kind of leadership. But their new president had no clue, presiding over one disastrous business decision after another, until the company had to be sold. The company that bought it closed it after a year, and moved the entire operation to its home base.

The unqualified son, although a nice enough guy, was naive. He unfortunately was under the impression that running a mature and complicated business required nothing more than ambition and personality. And his father was equally naive, failing to appreciate how a major family-before-business decision could be so disastrous. It was disastrous for the son, who now feels like a failure. Disastrous for the rest of the family, who are now denied ongoing financial returns. Disastrous for the employees, who were investing their own time and talent in the company as though it were their own. And disastrous to the community, whose economic base was eroded. Stakeholders all, and all lost.

There is the safety-net privilege that tempts some families to forget that their businesses are a responsibility. They use their companies as an employer of last resort, a make-work agency in the private sector.

A founder of a successful grocery chain hired his son-in-law because his daughter married below the lifestyle to which she had become accustomed. The founder of an auto parts distributorship bought up companies for his children to run, because they could not command elsewhere the salaries and bonuses he meted out. One founder, who owned several radio stations, created more and more non-core business divisions, like a printing company and a marketing firm, for each of his children to manage, ignoring the needs of the core business in the process.

The founder of a large auto dealership rescued his prodigal son from the big city where he had lost his low-end job in the entertainment world. The son was given a head sales position in mid-November, just in time to be included in the year-end bonus. At his father's insistence, and to the consternation of the hard-working older brother, and to the disgust of all other sales personnel, the new kid on the block got the same size bonus as those who had earned it since January 1.

The employees of a family-owned civil engineering company did not have the heart to ask the three remaining founders to move out of their much needed offices, where they usually napped two hours every morning and two hours in the afternoon. When they were not napping, they disrupted employees at their cramped work stations with diverting, idle chatter. No one wanted to kick them out of their offices. Everyone appreciated how, had it not been for these three warriors, no one would be working there. But still . . .

> *Why can't they be told to use the lounge? We're so desperate for space. Each of their offices would hold four of us. But around here it's the Golden Rule—the brothers in their golden years with all their gold can slow us all down. We end up taking care of them instead of taking care of business. Trouble is we like them. They're family to us, too. But they're in the way. It's sick to be waiting for them to die just to get their office space. It comes with being a family business.*
>
> Kate, age twenty-six, accounts receivable

There is also the home-away-from-home privilege. Some families use their businesses as extensions of their personal lives. The hot-headed father/son team of a marketing company regularly continued their weekend battles on Monday mornings at the office. The father's litany: the son's disorganization, his refusal to rescue his divorcing sister, and his being overweight. The son's litany: father's meddling with his daughter's personal life, the father's disorganization, and the father working on his golf game rather than becoming computer literate. Their office staff in the break room would lament . . .

> *How about a little less entertainment around here? Why don't they leave their family and personal crap out of the office? This is a business, for crying out loud!*

One husband/wife team that had started a software company allowed their marriage patterns to spill over into the office. When they were not speaking to each other, nobody in the office approached either one of them, even with legitimate business issues. When they snapped at each other in meetings, everyone shut down, mechanically finishing the agenda. When the husband hired someone with more skill sets than his spouse, in her department no less, and without her knowledge, let alone her input and consent, the new hire, of course, got caught in the middle, effectively rendering the department ineffective. Lunch time talk usually centered on what the staff called, "today's soap opera episode."

> *Either she should go work elsewhere so she can blossom, or he should start another business just for himself. Or they both should agree that our company is not their home battleground. Even when they are discussing normal business, they can end up yelling at each other, as though they are home. For them, unprofessional conduct at work is O.K. Disrespectful behavior has no place in the workplace. Let's start running this place like a business.*

When families refuse the discipline of leaving their personal lives at the door, they forget that families may be blind at times, but the employees are not.

There is also the perceived hands-off privilege. Nonfamily employees in such family businesses perceive a hands-off sign on some family members.

The nonfamily chief administrative officer of a medical supply company would not risk what she felt would be a career limiting conversation were she to go the president about late reports from his wife's finance department.

> *Who wants to be part of their pillow talk? Not me. There is not one signal around here that we can openly discuss needed improvements if either of them is involved.*

The sales personnel of a mortgage brokerage company reported to the oldest son of the owning family, who had recently been passed over for the president position. His retiring father selected his very capable middle son for the top spot. The oldest son went into a funk. What made matters worse was his management style—he was a top-down, micromanager. At a management retreat the managers refused to speak up about their frustrations. They felt they could not meet the projected numbers, because of the type of leadership they were being given. During breaks at the retreat, however, they talked openly about their new president, whom they regarded as their only hope.

> *Maybe he'll expect his older brother down the line to perform like he expects all the rest of us to perform. But family is family, and we gotta put up with it. Another lousy year ahead, and we're the ones who'll be held accountable. We'll see if the new president has got what it takes. Poor guy, he has to fill his old man's shoes, and pamper his older brother at the same time. Good luck.*

A large family-owned dairy was lucky enough to have a longtime loyalist working for them. He made a career of being a buffer. He was the buffer between the family members themselves, and between the family and the rest of the company.

*Everybody comes to me because they can't, or actually won't, go to each other. The owner confides in me about the kids; the kids confide in me about their dad; employees complain to me about the family, especially about all their privileges, and how they exclude all outsiders from any decision making. The family bellyaches to me about the employees' attitudes. I spend all my time dancing in between them all. If I didn't, I'm afraid all hell would break loose. My tombstone will read, "Here lies Mr. Buffer. He gave his life to someone else's family business." Some career, huh?*

This litany of privileges in no way implies that all family businesses indulge in self-serving privileges at the expense of their success. The temptations, however, are strong enough for every family business to heed Drucker's advice—"the family serves the business." Although the extreme of this advice is equally problematic (discussed in chapter 5), it is clear that family businesses can be rough places to work for family and nonfamily employees, especially when family matters interfere, or overwhelm business matters. A family business cannot flourish for long if family privileges sap its potential.

## SEPARATION OF HOME AND WORK

The primary responsibility of family owners is to run the business as a business. This requires the realization that a successful business, unlike a family business riddled by immediate privileges, will benefit the family in the long run immeasurably more when family matters are not allowed to mess things up at work. This requires a disciplined commitment to the separation of work and home. The needs of each can best be met when families doing business together appreciate what distinguishes work from home.

Work is where we solve problems for the rewards of the marketplace. Home is where we provide the closeness needed by each family member to grow as unique persons. Work is about merit. Home is about acceptance. Work is unsentimental. Home is sentimental. Because work is about results, family members are not to be indulged. Because family is about love, family members are not set up for failure when they work in the family's business.

## SUMMARY

Because a family's business is a responsibility, family matters have no business role in the workplace. Family matters can too easily ruin a family business. It behooves families in business together to establish a boundary between work life and home life. At work, everything needs to be professional in order to be successful. And being successful is the responsibility of the family owners. Home, while it too is a responsibility, is the place of privileges.

## BACK TO THE BASICS

1. List five things you do to insure that your business is run strictly as a business.
2. List four things you have done to convince family members that their work in the family business is strictly a responsibility.
3. What privileges do family members have in your family's business that other employees do not have?
4. How have you made sure that everyone in your company behaves professionally?
5. Identify one sentimental decision in your family's business that you have made for the sake of a family member—a decision you are glad you made, and would do again, if you had it to do over.

## CHAPTER THREE

# What's Best for Our Business?

*I don't want to take anything away from my father. What he did, starting with a pickup truck and two grocery stores, and ending up at the time of his death with a statewide distribution network and umpteen eighteen wheelers, will always be remarkable. But I'm here to tell you, business was easier then. Now we've got national competitors right in our backyard. We're dealing with purchasing pros, not some guy who understands produce. The old margins are gone. Customers are demanding greater variety. Ethnic groups are new markets we barely understand. And employees don't work like they did years ago. So we're changing, changing the way we do business all the way around. We've got to. There's no choice, if we want to survive and even succeed. My dad would've never done the stuff we're doing, like going after national accounts, or getting our employees' ideas. But he would approve. We're having to be as progressive today as he was in his day. He didn't stick with just one pickup truck, either.*

Doug, age fifty-four,
owner, wholesale produce company

ACCEPTING THE FAMILY BUSINESS AS A RESPONSIBILITY, rather than as a privilege, fundamentally means treating the business as though it were not a family business at all. It is a business with all the requirements and demands of nonfamily businesses. It is a business that has passion for results, and passion for results-producing employees, regardless of surname. It is a business that dedicates all its attention and resources to the best practices of business, as have the most successful family businesses over the years, such as Levi Strauss, Herman Miller, Marriott, Motorola, and WalMart.

It is questionable how dedicated many family businesses are to business best practices. The statistics cited previously suggest dedication to things other than to business best practices: seven of ten family businesses do not survive into the second generation; two of the three remaining do not survive into the third generation; and the typical family business has an average life span of only twenty-four years. Faced with such daunting odds, every family business person needs to be constantly guided by the question, "What's best for our business?"

## BUSINESS BEST PRACTICES

Although a thorough discussion of best practices is beyond the scope of this book, there are several best practices on the wish list of anyone who cares about family businesses. These best practices are mostly common sense, are well beyond management fads, and are not rocket science to practice. Unfortunately, they are seldom mentioned in the same breath with family businesses.

### Leadership

The first and most determining business best practice is effective leadership. In this day and age, leadership is more earned than given, by a long shot. It is best to think of leadership not as a position of prestige, but as a job and a relationship.[1] What I have seen all too often in family businesses is leadership defined by position, title, family name, and personality. I have also seen leadership relegated to the nice-to-have category, because it is not seen as important, compared to paperwork at the desk, for example, or community work. I appreciate that a young company in early start-up will have an entrepreneur as its leader, and that that style of leadership is mostly personality driven. I appreciate, too, that a second, third, or fourth generation family business will require a professional leadership team, in contrast to one dominant person, to lead an infinitely more complex organization. Leadership style thus varies depending on the age, size, complexities of the organization, and what business the organization is in. But virtually any organization needs the basic jobs of leadership to be done effectively.

### The Jobs of Leadership

- Position the company to meet the needs of customers in the marketplace
- Build a sound and flexible organization that can produce the goods and services needed by its customers
- Bring out the best in all the organization's employees
- Make happen what ordinarily wouldn't happen, to prevent "this is how we always do it" from stifling the organization
- Establish relationships with customers and employees based on trust, respect, honesty, and accountability
- Balance and prioritize competing interests and needs, for the good of the organization over the long haul
- Set the example of service—leaders are to serve, not be served

This job description requires persons who can gain followers. The simplest definition of leadership, after all, is someone who has earned followers. Followers are earned by persons who demonstrate character, talent, skills, experience, common sense, passion for other's success, energy, and have time to run the organization. Followers are earned by treating employees with respect, especially valuing their role and contributions. Followers are earned by someone whom employees can look up to.

Family businesses deserve and need this kind of effective leadership. When the family serves the business, the family owners hire and groom persons for leadership who can get the above jobs done, relating to people in a manner that earns their following. Last names are not important when it comes to the long term success of the business. Effective leadership is.

### A Unifying Controlling Philosophy

A second characteristic of successful companies involves a unifying controlling philosophy that articulates to customers and employees alike what the company is all about and what it stands for.[2] A unifying controlling philosophy means that everyone in the company works with a knowledge and understanding of the company's foundation. This foundation is built with organizational building blocks.

### Organizational Building Blocks

- The company's purpose
- The company's vision of the future
- The company's values that call for behavior of the highest common denominator
- The company's standards, requirements, and expectations of performance
- The company's accountability measures

Using these organizational building blocks, the company works to translate its philosophy into reality. Since successful, admirable businesses like 3M, Johnson & Johnson, Merck, and Hewlett-Packard have utilized this approach to doing business, family businesses anywhere can adopt and adapt a similar approach as well.

Family businesses would do well, as a start, to clearly articulate, as a matter of priority, the first and third organizational building blocks: the purpose of their business, and the values they wish to work by. These two building blocks help unify the company's workers, and help lift work relationships to a higher level.

The first organizational building block that family businesses need to create is a clearly spelled out, and widely understood, purpose—a purpose greater than their own family's immediate needs. Without a compelling purpose that drives all company activities, customers eventually will go elsewhere, and employees will end up as self-serving as the owners—a prescription for not making it into the next generation.

A very successful family farm has as its purpose, "We want to help feed and clothe people." Its management decisions, long range planning and work quality reflect this purpose. A family-owned food exporter has as its purpose, "We add variety to diets around the world." A family-owned millworking company has as its purpose, "Everything we do is for creating good jobs. We're part of the solution, not the problem." A family-owned trucking firm's purpose is "Helping other companies succeed by being the link between them." A family accountancy firm articulates its purpose as, "We deliver peace of mind." Purposes such as these shape and guide how the family does business, establish how the business is a long range responsibility, and lift all employees' work to a level of personal fulfillment.

Too many family businesses have a nonunifying, but very controlling philosophy. It translates essentially into, "We are the owners, and you're not." The corollary of this is equally uninspiring and unmotivating: "Since we are the owners, we control everything." This results in family members being the only ones in the company who can say yes to anything, with everyone else only being able to say no, as in "It's not up to us. It's not our business. You know, 'they who have the gold. . . .'" Would that every family business owner could say what Sam Walton said of WalMart: "We are led from the top, and run from the bottom." Too many family businesses are bossed from the top, and run from the top, the result of a guiding philosophy that is family centered only.

The other organizational building block requiring priority is company values. Family businesses need to practice business values that match their own personal values, whereby all employees are lifted to a higher standard of conduct. If the owners practice honesty, fairness, respect, kindness, generosity, and hard work in their personal lives, for example, why not have these same values practiced at work as well, by everyone? Some of the most admirable family businesses I know are extensions of the families who founded them—good people who figured that being good, and doing good, applied to work as much as it applied to personal life. They didn't buy the cheap ethic that there is a difference between personal values and business values. Separating the two gets translated into "Personal values are private and kinda soft. But business is business. It's dog eat dog. Watch your back side. Squeeze customers and vendors when you can. It's win/lose out there. So you gotta be hard, or you won't survive."

Conducting a business with values at the core requires a special type of toughness—the courage of conviction. For example, the owner/founder of a family trucking firm deeply felt that personal ethics and business ethics were one and the same:

> *The toughest decision I ever made was to say no to my biggest customer in the early going when we were struggling to get started and make ends meet. They asked us to do something shady to benefit them in exchange for continued business. They dumped us after I said no. But you know, as I look back, there really was no other choice. A clear conscience was more important than that one account, no matter how much we needed it. And the thing is, it wasn't too much later that we landed an even bigger account and have been flourishing ever since. Thank God and knock on wood.*
> Richard, age sixty-eight, founder and
> chairman, trucking company

This gentleman did not have to explicitly spell out his values for his company to follow. It was a small company, his example permeated the atmosphere, and his generation shared similar values. Today his son has had to spell out in detail the company's values and a code of behavior to go with it. The company is now so much larger and more complex. And we live in an era when most people lack a behavior compass at work, as though the lowest common denominator behavior, like street ethics or the ethical violations in big places that grab headlines, are what is needed to get ahead.

Family businesses have a real advantage when it comes to values behavior in their workplace—they can extend the values they want for their children and grandchildren right into their companies, making it incumbent on all employees to practice being their best selves while on the job.

## Customers in the Driver's Seat

Another crucially important business best practice is the pursuit of quality to satisfy customer demands. Customers have evolved from victims of obsolescence to kings, and now to dictators. The customer now defines quality of product and service. The customer practically determines price! And customer loyalty is a thing of the past. Many have observed that what has enabled American business to eventually compete with high-quality, low-cost international products and services has been a radical devotion to customer wants and needs. Providing customers defect-free products, and hassle-free services with warranties—no questions asked—is the way to do business today. Perhaps the only way.

Family businesses have to be as sophisticated as any global competitor in the use of quality techniques and cost-cutting techniques (Total Quality Management, or TQM, and Reengineering are but two of the more publicized approaches). Everything a family business does has to be aligned toward satisfying the customer. This is a difficult task, since customers are moving targets, and a father's customers will not necessarily transfer their loyalty to the son's and daughter's company.

Thus the never ending challenge of finding new customers and hanging onto them. When the family serves the business, the family owners focus all work activity on the customer, not on each other. There is no time for anything else.

## Employees As Partners

Another best practice of successful companies is pushing responsibility and decision making to the employees who are closest to the customer, and closest to the problems needing solution. This practice has several sources.

It owes to the fact that nothing motivates like responsibility. The more complete responsibility employees have, the more responsible they become. They then own their work. Also, successful companies appreciate their employees' ability to think and to come up with good ideas. They find their employees more than willing to share their thinking and suggestions when encouraged. Unlike anyone in management, employees have intimate working knowledge of the day-to-day details, upon which delivery of products and service to customers depend. Employees realize what is needed where the rubber meets the road. Employees also have more information at their disposal, thanks to information technology. Further, it is too slow and costly to wait for the chain of command to decide or solve something. What this adds up to for successful companies is the practice of running the company from the bottom, to use Sam Walton's phrase.

Employees no longer need to be seen as adversaries or second-class citizens. It is best to see them first as persons deserving the opportunity to succeed. The leadership in winning companies approach employees with the winning attitude, "I want you to succeed, I want to succeed, I want all of us to succeed."

Effective leadership also regards employees as partners, and as partners, the single most valuable asset a company has. Competitors have the same market requirements and access to the same technology, capital, labor pool, and distribution systems. What distinguishes the winners is their ability to work with their employees as partners, coordinating and utilizing their peoples' skills and efforts. These companies realize that without well equipped partners, the purpose of the company will not be fulfilled.

These companies spend a lot of time and effort making sure everyone is clear about priorities, especially the first priority—satisfying the customer. They equip their people through training and cross training. They keep their people informed, because people do poorly when kept in the dark. They teach them the financial realities of business, because every person in a company needs to be a business person, not just a few at the top. Employees working for such companies can thus be trusted with responsibility and decision making for taking care of the customer.

Too many family businesses that are not run as businesses tend to have an "us versus them" approach. They do not see employees as partners, since they are not family. They are viewed as not having much at stake, as though somehow their need to make a living, and find meaning in work, pales in comparison to the needs of the founding family. In effect, a self-centered family business approaches its employees with the losing attitude, "We want to succeed; your success doesn't really much matter." Such a family business forgets the benefits of having others, as partners, on its side.

### Merit-Based Rewards

One more business best practice that family businesses would do well to adopt is merit rewards. Successful companies increasingly link employment and reward to merit. Companies simply cannot compete and win in the global economy by reinforcing an entitlement mentality, whether at the executive level or at the front line. Businesses cannot afford private sector welfare, cannot be adult day care centers, cannot undermine work satisfaction by rewarding nonperformers, and cannot afford to lose their best employees by rewarding them the same as the subtracters.

Successful companies are diligent in giving meaningful performance feedback to all employees, including their leaders. Written performance feedback forms are developed for the company as a whole, for each area of the company, and for each employee. The feedback usually covers:

- Data about the customers' experience with the company; customers are visited, called, and surveyed for their experience with the company
- Feedback from peers and leaders for every partner on how well he or she has lived the company's values
- Measurements of performance regarding agreed-upon goals, including individual, department, and company-wide targets
- Goal setting for the next year
- Guidance for continued career development

Performance feedback, on a formal basis, is usually an annual event, with half-year follow-ups done during informal sessions with a partner's leader and/or during a team meeting.

Successful companies are diligent in giving performance feedback, not just twice a year, but on a regular basis, when good work or poor outcomes warrant attention. Leaders of the company, from frontline supervisors to the top executives, receive special training and coaching on how to give both formal, written, and informal, verbal feedback to recognize, help, and motivate all partners, including the leaders.

Employees measuring up are rewarded with continued employment. Those exceeding goals and expectations receive bonuses. Those falling short are coached to better performance. Those not willing to perform are told to work at a company better suited to their own standards.

All this is in stark contrast to traditional practices, ones too often found in family businesses. Traditionally, employees usually do not receive performance feedback at all, something employees repeatedly ask for in every company I have consulted. When traditional performance feedback is at least done, it too often is not helpful or motivating. Companies lazy about meaningful performance feedback generally practice across-the-board pay raises. This one-size-fits-all "reward for working here" is seldom appreciated. It has come to be expected, regardless of the company's success, with winners, nonwinners, and losers "rewarded" equally. Without a merit ethic, and without meaningful performance feedback, these companies are easily accused of practicing favoritism and nepotism.

Running a company on merit is fundamentally fairness in action. Valuable employees realize that it is what they do, and not who they are or whom they know, that should count for employment, promotion, and rewards. Family businesses, by becoming merit-based companies, would be placing family matters at work where they belong—at the door. When the family serves the business, the family owners employ and reward workers the old-fashioned way: the employees earn it, regardless of last name. Just like the founder of the family business earned success when he or she got started.

## SUMMARY

The overall guiding question for family businesses is the same as for any business: "What's best for the business?" When family business owners accept the responsibility of running a truly competitive, successful company, they leave family matters at the door. They concentrate on what it takes to not only keep customers, but also gain new ones. They accept the realities of success in the new economy. This means incorporating best practices of business into the daily work of their family's business.

## BACK TO THE BASICS

Hold a series of meetings with family members, both those inside and outside the company, and with employees, and ask the following questions. Create action steps for those things you agree need improvement.

1. How well do we execute the different leadership jobs for our organization?
2. Are we relating to our people in ways that earn their following?
3. What do we work for (purpose)?
4. What kind of company do we want to be down the road (vision)?
5. What do we stand for (values)?
6. How are we going to do business (standards, requirements, expectations)?
7. What are the consequences (accountability)?
8. Is everything we do focused on serving our customers with the best possible products and most satisfying service we can possibly provide?
9. Do our employees feel a partnership with us?
10. Have we equipped them to get the job done with minimal oversight?
11. Do we run our business on merit, or entitlement and privilege?

## CHAPTER FOUR

# The Family at Work

*Why can't he listen, just once? If there's one thing that really burns me up it's that he won't listen. After all the years I've been at this, I oughta know what the hell I'm talking about! But no, he does things his own way, not benefiting from what I all went through. I'm just trying to spare him the mistakes I made.*

Myron, age sixty-nine, second generation farmer,
referring to his forty-year-old
son, Larry

*Dad made a big deal of his retirement announcement. He got all the employees together, climbed up on a pile of pallets, and said it was time for him to hand over the reins to me. People applauded and then came up to me to wish me good luck. Dad took mom on a world cruise, came back a month later, and operated as though he never announced his retirement. Employees are confused—who do they report to? And I'm caught between a rock and a hard place: if I do nothing, I'll be miserable; if I have it out with Dad, we'll both be miserable. Now I don't know how to work with my own father.*

Jason, age thirty-six, new president of
engine remanufacturing company

*I never dreamed my son and I would ever work together, let alone work together so well. He's like a Pentium chip—smart, fast, organized, on top of things, reliable. He has really embraced this company. He's pulled the whole company up to a new level, including me. Especially computerizing everything. I actually now work more for him than he works for me. When I watch him with our people and see him so professional and effective, I get a lump in my throat. My son, the leader. Thank God.*

Leon, age fifty-three, owner, international
commodity brokerage firm

ALL THE TALK, ALL THE BOOKS, ALL THE SEMINARS, and all the meetings about business best practices will only benefit a family business when the family itself has a good on-the-job working relationship amongst themselves. It is how the family approaches each other and how their members get along with each other on the job that makes or breaks a family's endeavor.

Successful family businesses approach daily work with each other with twin goals in mind. The first is to foster each other's growth. The second goal is to get along with each other in a professional manner on a daily basis. Both goals create a mind-set in the family's business that says, "I want you to succeed, I want us to succeed, I want to succeed."

## FOSTERING GROWTH

Every business, family or not, has to develop its workforce in order to truly succeed. Raw talent is inadequate. Good intentions are not enough. Academic training needs to be seasoned with experience, guidance, further training, and big league demands and pressures. Skills and approaches that were good enough yesterday are not good enough in the new economy. What worked when the company was a start-up is seldom effective when the company is a larger, more complex organization. The command-and-control leadership of the entrepreneur founder needs to be replaced in a larger organization by leadership that increasingly relies on and maximizes the skills of a talented workforce that works well together. Larry Bossidy, President/CEO of Allied Signal, recently put it this way: "At the end of the day, we bet on people, not strategies."[1]

Family businesses have an added challenge that nonfamily businesses do not have. In addition to cultivating their nonfamily workforce, they have the added responsibility of fostering the growth of their own flesh and blood. This responsibility has to be a goal of highest priority, especially during the first and second generations when family businesses are typically so dependent on family players.

### Fostering Children's Growth at Work

It is imperative for parents in family business to be certain that their children want to work in their family's enterprise. They also need to be certain that their children are well prepared to contribute to the success of the business.

Children will want to work in their family's business when, from a young age on, they see and hear their parents' love and passion for their work. Love and passion for their work has always distinguished successful people. They pour their hearts and souls into their work, in addition to their time and money. They are charged and recharged by their dream, their challenges, the people they deal with, the results and rewards of their efforts. They talk a lot about their adventures. They tell war stories of the past, stories of remarkable people, stories of turning points and close calls, stories of success and mistakes. These stories always reveal the values of the family at work, values that can lift children's natural aspirations. And of course, children have a sixth sense similar to good dogs: they can sense what is going on, including whether or not their parents have enthusiasm for their business. If they do, then the business becomes attractive to the children.

The reverse of this is also true. Too many family-business people bring home the garbage of work. Talk at home is nothing but negatives. This went wrong, that went wrong. There is this potential crisis or that potential crisis that will bring ruin. Employees, too many of them, are just out for themselves; they cannot be trusted, so they must be enemies. Competitors definitely are enemies. The government is enemy number one. Going to work Monday morning is biting into the sour apple, getting into the harness, and getting on the treadmill and going nowhere. A steady diet of this griping and complaining about the family's business is hardly motivating for children to pattern themselves after their parents. Except for feeling sorry for their parents, and wanting to eventually join the family business in order to rescue their pitiful parents, children will hardly develop a love and passion for the business they eventually might own.

Parents need to curb their frankness in front of the children about the darker moments of business until children emerge from their most formative years with an appreciation of their parents' love and passion for work. Family-business people almost always do love their work, and maintain the passion of their dream for tomorrow. They need to admit this, and be proud of it. Getting this across to children repeatedly will foster inspired future partners. Children ten years of age and older can better absorb some of the harder realities of business, and learn how problems are challenges to be met, when they see and hear their parents behave and speak well of the family's work.

If children show interest in the family's work, it is a good practice to introduce them to the actual work within the company. Early in a child's life this means bringing them to work, showing them around, introducing them to employees and equipment, dazzling them with the importance of what the company actually contributes to the broader world. Later on, usually during adolescence, this can mean summertime employment, preferably under the supervision of a trusted nonfamily employee who is motivated to foster the teenager's growth, rather than "babysitting the boss's kid who'll someday be bossing me around." This work experience is best spoken of as "an apprenticeship with good mentoring." It can prove advantageous later on when a child chooses a career in the family's business.

By the time children complete high school, they should be crystal clear about the education and work experience expected of them if they desire to work for the family's business.

One of the successful family businesses I have worked with adhered to their founding father's rule: a graduate degree and six years experience working elsewhere before any of the children can work for the family's farm. Two other successful family businesses I consulted invited a son in one case, and a grandson in the other, to join the families' work only after the young men had passed their bar exams and had successfully practiced business law. These young men brought their success from elsewhere, their legal knowledge of contracts and corporate governance, their own work ethic, and their respect for continuing education and learning to their families' businesses. Good hires, both, regardless of their last names.

The profound shaping that education and outside work experience can have on young adults will produce exactly what the family business needs in the future. These young people will be informed, independent thinkers who have discovered what they are interested in and what they are good at. They will be workers who bring independent, realistic confidence from working with people in other walks in life. They will be employees who will bring to their family's company what works and does not work elsewhere. And they will bring their own aspirations, aspirations that can lift and carry the company into the new day.

What follows education and outside experience is a broadbased experience within the company. The military's approach to fostering the growth of leaders is a good role model for family businesses. No one is made colonel, let alone general or admiral, fresh out of boot camp or military school. Promising young men and women receive assignments in many very different services and locations in order to develop expertise in a variety of disciplines, and to develop a feel for the whole. All this before becoming responsible for the whole.

The next generation of family-business leaders needs to have stints of service, apprenticeships actually, in practically all aspects of the business. They need to spend time, for example, in production and operations, in marketing, in sales, in finances, in frontline supervisory roles, and especially in face-to-face work with customers. They need to experience the family's business from the bottom up in order to someday effectively lead it from the top, while allowing it to be run from the bottom.

Children's professional growth would further be developed during these apprenticeship years if they had a good mentor. Good mentors are preferably mature, experienced nonfamily employees who are at the point in their careers where they get a kick out of fostering other's growth. They are no longer competitive and self-serving. Rather, they know how important it is for a young worker to have someone invested in his or her success, someone who listens with understanding, someone who will "clue the kid in" on how things really work in the company, someone who will clue the employees in that the kid is all right, and someone who will clue the parents in that indeed the kid is going to be just fine.

A good mentor, of course, will be tough on the young adult if the situation warrants it. Mistakes are to be learned from and forgiven. Risk taking is to be encouraged. But growth cannot be fostered if areas of improvement are ignored or attitudes inappropriate to success are not dealt with in a straightforward manner. My own father still chuckles over an incident with the boss's son who told my dad that he did not have to do something because of who he was: "Do you know who my dad is?" To which my father replied, "I sure do. Why don't we just waltz over to his office right now and tell him all about this. We'll see who he thinks you are." My dad claims he never had a minute's worth of trouble with the son again. The son, incidentally, declined the trip to his dad's office.

It is easier to foster the growth of a young family member if he or she reports to nonfamily supervisors or managers. It underlines in daily behavior how the family means business. Home is home. There family members "report" to each other. Work is work. Here family members report to someone free of the family's emotional baggage. This way the young family member can be an employee earning a living, earning others' respect, and learning the ropes to assume bigger responsibilities in the future.

Some family businesses even go so far as to start separate businesses or create autonomous divisions for each of their children.

They wisely want to avoid sibling conflict, sure, but more importantly, they want to preserve family ties in personal life. This fosters growth both at work and at home. One family business I worked with insisted that any child or grandchild wanting to join their business had to, as a condition of employment, come up with a new product line to manage, and for which they would have bottom line responsibility. This new product had to be approved by the company's executive team, which included nonfamily managers. Approval was based on the soundness of the business plan, the thoroughness of the market research, and the preparedness of the young family member. Too demanding? No, just part of fostering children's growth, rather than setting them up for lackluster careers crippled by an entitlement mentality.

### One of the Best Teachers

Families that want to foster their children's growth at work need to utilize one of the most effective teachers there is—experience with feedback.

Experience without feedback only goes so far. Sure, you can get pretty good at something on your own, but it is the rare person who can truly become an expert without the invaluable help of feedback from observers, customers, experts, or those affected. Companies that throw their employees off the bridge into the deep, fast water of demanding work, without giving continuous feedback on how to swim, let alone survive, are companies with high turnover rates, low productivity, and nonloyal, frustrated employees. Long before total frustration sets in, these employees ask for more training and performance feedback that is helpful and motivating. Employees know that there are almost always better ways to do things, bad habits to eliminate, lessons to be learned, and new approaches and technology to be absorbed. They appreciate that self-discovery does not take them as far as they would like to go.

Two industries, neither the province of family businesses, have practically perfected the use of experience with feedback to promote the growth of its professionals and participants. One is the entertainment/recreation world. A musician or actor seldom achieves stardom, or even conscious competence, without the use of feedback from coaches, who use recordings and videotape as feedback tools. Football teams are famous for Monday reviews of weekend game films. Baseball hitters and pitchers are continuously going over videotapes with their coaches in order to perfect their techniques. The weekend golfer is forever asking golfing buddies, "Now what the hell am I doing wrong?" after slicing yet another ball out of bounds. No fly fisherman ever got into the elite 10 percent who catch 90 percent of the fish without feedback from really expert fly fisherman (and the fish!). Skiers seldom can achieve a relaxed, fluid style that enables them to ski the black diamond runs (the steepest and most exciting) unless their experience is informed by feedback of those more skilled.

The other industry is health care. Health care generally does an excellent job of fostering the growth of its new practitioners by using experience with feedback. Young physicians during the three to five years after medical school are groomed to be successful health care providers by experiencing thousands of patients with hundreds of different ailments and needs. All these experiences become teaching opportunities for the cast of coaches that populate medical training. Young doctors have senior doctors accompany them when seeing patients—someone looking over their shoulders (treated as sin in the business world). Feedback after patient visits is geared to make sense of the experience. In addition, young doctors have to record what they see, what they think, what they decide and why, and what the outcomes are—making a record of every patient visit they experience. This documentation is in itself a learning tool, but it is also a tool for the teaching physicians when they audit the young doctors' progress and care of patients. The charts are also used for presentations at meetings where everyone learns from each other. They are also used as records of competence to qualify physicians for solo practice and hospital privileges. Videotaping of physicians in training is increasingly being used, so that technical skills and people skills are enhanced by more than just experience alone. The tapes are carefully gone over with the young physicians by experts giving feedback.

I belabor this point about experience with feedback as being one of the best teachers there is anywhere because the business world does not use it nearly enough. Typically, businesses practice the "sink or swim," "trial by fire," "school of hard knocks" approach to (non)grooming their employees: "There's your desk; we use Windows 95; there's a file for phone numbers; good luck." Or, "Here's your forklift truck; pick up the keys from the foreman every morning; we don't want damaged product, so cool it on the corners; now get going." Following this "orientation" the employee is left to his or her own devices to become an expert with little or no helpful feedback.

Since experience with feedback is a good enough teacher for the entertainment/recreation world and the health care field, it is surely good enough for family businesses. In order to foster the growth of the next generation, family businesses have to make feedback a binding requirement of the organization to give, and a binding requirement of the young family-business person to receive and benefit from.

Some examples of experience with feedback will illustrate how it could work. A young family member in sales goes over with a very good senior salesperson the last five calls the young person has made. Topics to be discussed include relationship building, product knowledge, pricing, closing techniques, results, and follow-up. This same young salesperson would also have a coach along (yes, looking over his or her shoulder) on cold calls and sales presentations. Afterwards they would thoroughly review the experiences for learning. This is a family business that wants to foster its next generation's growth.

A young farmer would be required to keep seasonal records per crop, much like the physician's medical charts per patient. Annual records of seed varieties, depth at which they were planted, weather, soil testing, water and chemical usage, labor costs, equipment overhead, yields, harvest data, hauling costs, and market prices would all be used as teaching devices in their own right. These records also would be used for discussion with more experienced farmers and agriculture advisors. Experience with feedback, rather than experience in a vacuum, can be a binding requirement on a family farm that wants to thrive for another generation.

A mechanical engineer joining his family's manufacturing company would be required to regularly make presentations at weekly production meetings, quality control meetings, purchasing/inventory meetings, process mapping meetings, and/or sales meetings. His presentations would be about his own work, his team's work, and the department's work. He would be required to highlight what has been good, bad, and ugly, what can be done to get closer to zero defects, and how best to respond to customers in a customized, timely way. His presentations would be followed by feedback from coworkers, managers, coaches, and occasionally consultants. Feedback that is intended to foster the young engineer's growth in his own family's business.

One last example. A family business grooming a daughter to become its president/chief executive officer would require several things of her. She would have to seek leadership training and peer-leadership mentoring from outside of the company, especially by joining organizations dedicated to nurturing young leaders. She would be required to lead the company in its annual efforts to establish goals for the next year—goals for the company as a whole, and for each division, each department, and all key personnel. Her leadership in goal setting would always be accompanied by written and verbal feedback from those involved, as well as from family members in their capacity as owners. Additionally, she would be required to present business plans for new products, ventures, or acquisitions, whether for real or for practice. These presentations would be made to executives, frontline employees, board members, owners, and outside advisors like the family's banker, accountant, attorney, family business consultant, and market focus groups. Each of these presentations would be followed by feedback so that the president-elect can learn as much as possible about her readiness.

Since singers, quarterbacks, golfers, and doctors become professionals by experience enriched with feedback, the next generation of any family business can become national and even world-class business people if their families truly commit to fostering their growth from day one and continuing to do so throughout their careers.

## Fostering Parents' Growth at Work

Only when the economy is very favorable for business, like the 1980s, can companies succeed in spite of their leaders. Companies usually cannot succeed beyond the overall skills of its executive leadership. Leadership is the outer limits of a company's progress. That is why business leaders must continually grow, improve their skills, and take their people to higher levels of performance. In family business this means parents, who usually are in charge, must continue to grow professionally.

## Keeping Current

Founders and succeeding generations of executives of family businesses cannot lead their companies looking at things through glasses of previous decades. To approach everything with "this is the way we've always done it, and if it was good enough when we were driving Edsels, it's good enough now" simply is a prescription for the demise of another family business.

For parents, keeping current involves maintaining close contact with customers, especially key customers and potential new ones. Keeping current involves reading, reading about the economy, the industry, the changing market, the advance of technology, the products and services most in demand, and the organizational revolution of the past twenty years. Keeping current involves active participation in the many fine industry, professional, and trade associations geared to fostering the growth of their members. Keeping current involves active participation in community service, a sobering experience, usually, but one that teaches the need for persuasion and patience, and teaches the realities of the world around us. Keeping current involves frequent, informal get-togethers over a meal or a drink with fellow parents who undoubtedly are going through similar experiences, but who may have a best practice or two to learn.

Keeping current means attending leadership development courses and family business forums sponsored by universities and professionals, such as accountancy and legal firms, to incorporate more effective approaches. Keeping current also means the parents saying to themselves, "I want to keep improving. Everyday there's something new. I don't know it all. I've poured my heart and soul into all this, so I might as well keep pouring my mind into all this as well. I'll prove that an old dog can learn new tricks."

### Letting Go

Keeping current for parents, while relatively easy, is not, however, enough. The other absolutely essential part of fostering parents' growth at work is so much more difficult. It is the art of letting go. Parents in family business, over the length of their careers, have to learn to increasingly let go of trying to control everything in the companies they have founded or inherited.

It is ironic how business people decry the centralized, controlling influence of government while they continue to practice just that—centralized control over their own organizations. Granted, when the family's company is in its earliest stages, the founding father or mother does everything, doing so out of necessity. Granted also is the need of any company to be led by impassioned executives, regardless of the size of the company. But the issue of letting go (gracefully would be best) is the issue of growing an organization to a maturity that enables it to thrive, not only beyond the life of the founder, but also thrive day-to-day as he or she backs off of the nitty-gritty details in order to lead the big picture. As one chief executive officer told me about his job in a two-billion-dollar-a-year sales family business: "I have only two jobs—create a culture here so everyone can succeed, and make less and less decisions, reserving for myself only a few big ones that would have widespread impact on our success. The fewer decisions I have to make means more and more other people are making the decisions they are capable of making, and are paid to make. Basically, I hardly control anything around here anymore. I've made sure things are under control without me." This is a family business executive who has grown into his leadership job. He is not working at one, two, or three levels beneath his title, as is so often the case. He has made sure he has the right people in the right places doing their jobs, rather than robbing them of their jobs.

Parents in family business need to grow with the growth of their company. They need to hire well, make sure their people are guided by the company's purpose, values, direction, and current business goals, foster everyone's growth, including their children's, and then get out of the way.

Most executives, including too many in family businesses, do not get out of the way because they are unsure of themselves in their jobs at the top. This lack of confidence and certainty, when compounded by stressful situations, causes executives to go right back to what they are good at and most comfortable with—their old jobs, the jobs they were doing when things were smaller, simpler, and manageable. *Manageable* is the operative word here—they try to manage things from the top, rather than lead from the top and require the organization to run from the bottom.

Family business parents who continue to manage as though their companies still could fit around a small table, like in the good old days when things were fun, basically are saying to their employees, their own children included: "I don't know what to do now that the company is so big. So I'll do what I successfully did before. I want things my way. I only need you for doing what I say. I can still stay on top of thousands of details, believe me. I'll do the thinking, you do the work. I'll tell you not only what to do, but also how to do it. You're empowered, but pass everything by me first."

This lack of professional growth by family business leaders produces passive, dependent organizations that will always need training wheels to get anywhere. Everyone will be running around seeking permission, approval, and signatures. Everyone will use the words, "I'll have to check first and then get back to you; it's not up to me." The irony, of course, is that every so often a brave, aggressive, free-thinking employee will make an independent decision that the founder will find out about. The founder beams and says, "Now that's the kind of employee we need around here. He's a guy after my own heart." If only every employee were so courageous.

Imagine if that founder would make it known across the entire company that he or she wants everyone to be using their business sense and common sense to make decisions that go with their responsibilities. All that it would take to make it known across the company is the company's grapevine: "You know what the old man told Frank? He told him that he refuses to make decisions for us anymore. He said he would stop anyone from bankrupting the outfit, but other than that we're supposed to start being businesspeople ourselves. I've got to see it to believe it, but I might try it myself." Unfortunately, most employees are usually too afraid of either losing their jobs, or afraid of having their work life made miserable, to give the founder reason to make this speech. Instead they play "Mother, may I?" or "What should I do?"

My own father has a good grasp on his need to let go of controlling my brother's and my life. Ever since we were teenagers he would say, "Now that the boys are bigger than me I'll have to keep my mouth shut." Reminding him of this a couple hundred times or so has turned into a family joke. Even dad, when wanting his way so much on something that is clearly our call, ends up laughing. It is as though my father made the observation that life has two totally satisfying relationships: between best friends, and between grandparents and grandchildren. Neither relationship is handicapped by one trying to control the other.

Working relationships do not have to be controlled. They can be based on trust, respect, spirited discussion and debate, and accountability. People at work want to be treated as adults, including the adult children of the family owning the company. Outside of work people are responsible adults who raise nice families, keep nice homes, get their kids to school on time, go to religious services, pay their taxes and abide by the law. At work they are treated as kids needing to be controlled. This naturally is resented. They look to the family business leader to set a good example, set an intelligent course, create an atmosphere that promotes good work, and then get out of the way.

Family business leaders need to continue to grow with their companies. They best can do so by keeping current with the business world and current with their own organizations' needs. They also need to increasingly resist the temptation to control everything. When they foster their own growth in such ways they will garner the respect of everyone at work, including especially their own children who choose to work there.

## TEN GUIDELINES FOR GETTING ALONG WITH EACH OTHER

Just as it is true that job satisfaction of employees in any company is largely determined by their relationship to their immediate supervisor, family members' job satisfaction is largely determined by their family relationships. A daughter can love her work, but struggle with her father, to the point of wishing some days she could fire him. She ends up sour about getting up every morning and going to work at a place she even partially owns. A son can have everything going for him on the job except for an unprofessional working relationship with his brothers, and end up hating his work. A father can have every reason to be proud of his career, but be brokenhearted over the bickering, rejections, jealousy, and spitefulness his family displays to each other on the job. At times it crosses his mind to fire them all and start over with outsiders. Children can love the business as much as the founder, but want to fire their father if he continues to be controlling and meddlesome, while all the while claiming he wants them to be taking things over.

Successful family businesses work hard at preventing such tensions by pursuing the goal of getting along with each other at work in a professional manner on a daily basis. The goal is professional relationships. To get along with family members at work, families would do well to practice the following ten guidelines.

### Guideline One—Eliminate Personality Clashes

If personalities naturally clash, forget it. Forget about even trying to work together. Some personalities just clash. Usually it is family members who are either too similar to each other, or so different from each other that they just cannot get along. Often it is mismanaged sibling rivalry from yesterday. Whatever the cause, families wanting each of their members to succeed do not push square pegs into round holes. Business is challenging enough without the daily futility of making a mismatch work effectively together. Don't even try. They would be better off working somewhere else. The world is big enough to offer opportunities elsewhere for family members who deserve a good work experience. Getting along in personal life is a big enough challenge. Why force things at work?

### Guideline Two—Focus on Goals

Stay focused on big business goals. A family business needs to have clearly defined business goals that everyone supports and works toward. Big goals lift the spirit and commitment of everyone, especially when everyone participates in setting the goals. The work required to reach these goals is so demanding and encompassing that no one has time for being small. Someone once said, "In the absence of a great dream, people pursue petty things." In the absence of big goals and demanding work, family members can too easily waste time and energy on petty intrafamily things. Office politics is usually the province of underchallenged, bored, unproductive people anyway. Develop the family's big dream, and set big goals for everyone to meet, and family members will have to relate professionally.

### Guideline Three—Compartmentalize

Leave family matters at the door. When family members step foot on their company's property, they have to shift gears. It is the shift from being family members to being business professionals. It is "show time" when they come through the door. It is time to show the rest of the company that the family means business. They are on stage. Every employee in a family business is an expert family watcher anyway, so they need to be shown what dedicated, big-goal oriented work is all about. Psychologists talk about compartmentalizing: put personal stuff in one compartment, business stuff in another. Perform "as if" there are no family matters at work, only business matters. Family members get along with each other best when they in effect say to one other, "We've got a big job to do. Let's set any crappy stuff aside and get to work."

### Guideline Four—Eliminate Special Treatment

Treat each other as nonfamily employees. Some fathers, in an effort to avoid favoritism, are harder and coarser with their children than they are with other employees. Employees have little respect for this, ending up "feeling sorry for the kid." Some family members get a free ride. This is worst yet for the company. Some families huddle together by themselves in an office, something usually interpreted by the rest of the company as an exclusive club, or something to gossip about. Some families speak several languages. Whenever they resort to one not understood by the rest of the company, they invite paranoia all around: "They're talking about us. Something bad is being discussed." Some families shy away from saying something that the rest of the company is aching to say, something obvious about a family member's performance that simply needs to be dealt with. Were it about a nonfamily employee, things would be said and handled appropriately.

There simply is not any room in a family business to have family or family members singled out for treatment different than for others. Family membership has no privileges, or special burdens, at work. Just responsibility on the job like everyone else.

### Guideline Five—Praise and Correct Effectively

Praise in public, correct in private, cause no triangles. Two of the oldest pieces of supervisory wisdom, "praise in public, correct in private," apply to family members as well as to employees in general. Giving family members credit when credit is due is not in any way showing family favoritism. Family members will appreciate the recognition, and will be motivated by it. Nonfamily members, if they also receive timely recognition in front of others, will sense the fairness of a family member being praised for good work.

Correcting mistakes, poor performance, or poor behavior should never cause embarrassment in front of others. Corrections are for learning, and learning is nearly impossible when a family member tends, unlike a nonfamily member, to experience corrections as a replay of early home life, even when done effectively, adult to adult.

The third supervisory guideline, "cause no triangles," while applicable generally, is particularly important for family members needing to get along with each other professionally. Family members are easily tempted, because of familiarity, to blurt out things like, "Well, that's my brother, he is always . . . "; "You know my dad, he is never going to . . . "; "Is she at it again? I know, I know. I've had that same problem with my sister ever since we were kids." Family members should never disparage another family member behind his or her back. It creates a triangle with the persons being told. Triangles promote secrets, gossip, coalitions, and disrespect, including disrespect for the one doing the knocking. Nothing negative should be said without first, or as soon as possible, going to the family member directly and saying it face to face, adult to adult, in private. It is a matter of respect, trust, class, and commitment to mutual success.

## Guideline Six—Give Advice Carefully

Think before giving advice; think while receiving advice. Families usually feel they have a license to give each other advice. No other relationships exchange advice as freely as families do. Trouble is, few things trigger negative feelings quicker than advice giving: "This is what you should do"; "I don't want to tell you what to do, but . . . "; "If I were you, I would . . . "; "Listen to me for once. You'd be better off if you . . . "; "I've seen this type of thing a hundred times. I know better, believe me, I know. Here's how to handle it." These efforts, however well meaning, almost always are heard as the following: "You're dumb, I'm smarter"; "I'll do the thinking, which obviously is something you're not capable of"; "Do what I say!"; "You could never figure this out on your own, so I'll figure it out for you"; "Here, let me rescue you, you poor little thing"; "I'm the parent, you're still a child." Since advice is commonly experienced this way, it is usually not followed, or it is customized by the advisee beyond the advisor's recognition. This leads to the advisor's exasperation: "Why don't you listen for a change!" To which the advisee says a hundred times, "Yes, but . . ."

In order to get along with family members professionally, family members need to think before giving advice. It is best to think the following:

- Listen first for the other's take on the situation
- Trust the other's capacity to think
- Help sort out what is crucial and what is not
- Suggest what needs to be done, not how to do it
- Ask permission to offer your ideas
- Respect the other's right to make a mistake; mistakes can be excellent teachers, especially with constructive feedback

When receiving advice, family members would do well to think the following: "He's only trying to help"; "His intentions are good"; "She's only wanting to spare me some hard experiences"; "She is, after all, on my side"; "His style is overbearing, but I'll cut him some slack"; "I'll consider this advice and make something of it that's my own, but I'll show appreciation for his good intentions"; "I'll do it, even if it's her suggestion"; "This isn't worth a fight. I'll come back later and ask him when he cools off to just help me sort things out." Professional relationships deserve this thoughtfulness. After all, the purpose and big goals of the family business are too important to be derailed by some all too common advice exchanges.

### Guideline Seven—Use Persuasion

Use persuasion, rather than giving orders. No one wants to be ordered around. No one handles being ordered around very well. Family members, especially parents, are more susceptible to ordering family members around than they are nonfamily employees. It is the familiarity thing again. Or failure to appreciate the autonomous adulthood of children working in the company. Persuasion is the professional way of getting along with fellow workers, including family members.

Persuasion involves explanation of the rationale of something. It is explaining the desired outcome first. It is explaining the reasons for what is desired, the needs to be met, the importance of it all, the consequences of inaction and action. It is clear about what needs to be done, while respecting the other's need to figure out how. It is listening for the other's viewpoints. It is seeking partners, not obedient servants. It is being thorough enough ahead of time to prevent the disgruntled lament, "If he just would have taken a few minutes to explain things first, I would have understood and could've taken care of it."

## Guideline Eight—Treat Children Equally

Give each child equal attention whenever possible. Sometimes more than one adult child works in the family's company. When parents are also active in the business, it is important for them to make the rounds, giving each of their children as close to equal attention as possible. Frequently a parent and one particular child work more closely with each other. A father, the president, and his daughter, the accountant, for example, have offices next door. The son is in sales and consequently is on the road a lot. He only has sporadic contact with father. Father needs to think "sibling rivalry." It does not matter that the children are in their late thirties. Sure, they are more mature than twenty years ago. Sure, they do not believe they have a problem with each other anymore. Still, the father needs to think "sibling rivalry." It is thinly veiled in the son's statement, "I just keep clear. My sister has to work with dad. That's why she gets the big bucks, hah hah. That's fine with me. And she'll probably inherit more than me too, hah hah." The "hah hah" joking is a dead giveaway of sibling rivalry.

Sometimes adult sibling rivalry is not thinly veiled. It pops up as office guerrilla warfare. Father and son work in Company A.

Another son works in the family's Company B. Father bought B to keep the boys separate. He has had his office in A for years. It is home for him. It is where the family's business all began. So father hardly ever gets over to visit son in Company B. The finances of B, however, are run through Company A—it is large, well equipped, well staffed; and no one saw any need for duplication. No one saw finances, however, as the field on which a sibling rivalry game could be played. Feeling like an orphan, and seeing his company as an orphan to the "parent" company, son in Company B begins sending financial data days and then weeks late. He sends data that is not formatted for easy use, and data that is incomplete. Accounts receivable is not told about credit changes for several key customers. Payroll is not told of changes for several employees' benefits. The outside CPA firm is not sent quarterly tax data. Although there are excuses for all this, it is clear to any outsider that Company B son is playing a game, a game that finally gets him what he is looking for—attention from dad, albeit negative attention, just like old home week. Had father been visiting the Company B son, and shown more interest in what was going on over at Company B other than just its finances, he would have made it so much easier for his son to get along with his family in a professional, rather than childish, way.

## Guideline Nine—Be Grateful

Let gratitude for parents carry the day. Parents can be difficult, no doubt about it. This is just how it is between generations. It is nothing new or out of the ordinary. But parents do deserve some grace. Parents, like we all are, are products of their times and are more than likely doing the best they know how. And virtually every parent in family business has the very best of motivations—a dream of having a business for his or her children to run and own "so they and their kids will have it better than we ever had." Far too many children of family businesses forget all this. They forget about the blessing they have that most others do not have—inheriting a golden opportunity to succeed. While others start from scratch, children of family businesses start from second or third base, or start in the second period up by two goals. Of course they are not exempt from the hard work and perils that accompany business success. But what a start they have! What an opportunity. What a debt of gratitude is owed their parents who sacrificed, sweated, and risked all to be able to pass it along. As two brothers recently told me, "We work hard at getting along with each other. We feel we have an obligation to repay the opportunity given us. We're not going to tear down what our grandparents started, and what our parents worked so hard to build up. We owe them big time."

Gratitude is the foundation of ethics: "Where someone has been given much, much will be expected of him; and the more someone has had entrusted to him the more he will be required to repay" (Luke 12:48). The minimum requirement of gratitude owed parents in a family business is this: it is everyone in the family working hard to maintain professional working relationships with each other. For the sake of the parents. For the sake of the business.

### Guideline Ten—Stand Together

It is better to be close than to be right, most of the time. There are rare situations in family business when it is better to be right, no matter what. Getting along with each other should never supersede violations of the family's values, business ethics, the law, or professional conduct. Given these exceptions, however, it is better for family members to be guided by the family's need to be a family, and the need of the business to have a unified family behind it: "If a household is divided against itself, that house will never stand" (Mark 3:25). A family that chooses closeness between its members has a better chance by far to stand among those family businesses that succeed generation after generation.

### SUMMARY

A family business, in order to succeed, has to perform as though it were not a family business at all. It plays in the same league as do all other businesses. But it has the added challenges of family matters at home, and working together day in and day out.

To lighten the challenge and better pave the way to business success, families in business together need to observe two best practices. The first is to vigorously foster each other's growth, from members at a tender age to members past retirement. This goal is a supreme compliment. It shows commitment to each other, confidence in everyone's ability to learn and to grow, enthusiasm for each other's success, and an investment in the company's future.

The second best practice for family members working together is making concerted efforts to get along with each other in professional ways "as if" family members were regular employees. Ten guidelines are offered for getting along, all based on the premise that being family is no reason to behave badly, or treat each other poorly. What is good for all relationships, like respect, praise, uplifting goals, and gratitude, is good for family too.

## BACK TO THE BASICS

1. Conduct a skills inventory in your company by interviewing everyone for their views of the company's training and education needs. Based on these findings, what can a cross representational group of employees, including family members, make possible over the next twelve months to enhance the skill levels of your people?
2. Have a family discussion about what is perceived as the family's requirements and expectations of family members who want to join the company. Has everyone been well served by these requirements and expectations? Are they sufficient for the next generation?

3. Pick three or four mature, trustworthy employees and discuss with them the possibility of their becoming mentors to young people in your company, including young family members. Encourage them to take them under their wings once a week or so to just talk about how things are going.

4. Call a family meeting and discuss the desirability of using the "Ten Guidelines for Getting Along With Each Other" as your own guideline for the next six months. Six months later, use the guidelines for giving each other individual feedback in private.

# PART TWO
## The Family's Home Life

## CHAPTER FIVE

# What Could Be More Important Than Our Family?

*My brothers and sisters are all in agreement that our family busi-
ness caused our parents to divorce. We died as a family, while the
business made a fortune. Dad found the big time too exciting to be
a family man. And he found mom too plain and ordinary to fit his
nouveau riche lifestyle. He ran off with a trophy girlfriend, and
mom was left holding the bag with us kids. True, mom wouldn't
change her dislike of high society, so she gained a lot of weight to
protect herself, and to protest. And now I have to walk on thin ice
between my mom and my dad, with his new wife—I work for him
in our family business.*

Bruce, age thirty-one, salesman,
independent insurance agency

FAMILIES INVOLVED IN THEIR OWN BUSINESSES HAVE
in many ways the best of all worlds. They have the opportunity to
accomplish something important with people they live and die for.
They can accomplish something free of outside, absentee ownership.
They can accomplish something that will benefit grandchildren and
their children. And they can make their family name synonymous
with contributing to the economic well-being of their communities.
What a wonderful experience it is for some.

Trouble is, for other families in business together this best of all worlds has come at a terrible price. The price is almost always family neglect. In order to make the family business successful, families have sacrificed their private home life on the altar of their business. They serve the business in the extreme.

## THE DOMINANCE OF WORK

Work can easily dominate the priorities of anyone and any family, leaving little time, energy, or passion for anything else. Many factors are involved. Work does play such a critical role in life. It is sacred, an expression of our uniquely human gifts and talents. Work is psychological, fulfilling our needs to achieve, to be important, to make a difference. Work is necessary; there is no free lunch. Work is natural—just watch a two year old on the kitchen floor moving the world of Tupperware containers around. Work is fun; it is seductively engrossing and exhilarating when it provides challenge, risk, and reward. Work is demanding, absorbing energy, time, and mental preoccupation. And work is rewarding, its rewards much more immediate than family life can offer.

Then too, starting, owning, and running a business is no forty-hour-per-week exercise. A start-up company, especially, is a real slave driver. Extra help can't be afforded; the founders themselves often go without pay, plowing everything back into the business, while trying to repay banks and venture capital investors. This is not an uncommon way for more family members to get involved in the business—it is not easy to get outsiders to come in and work long hours for practically nothing in an outfit with no track record or security.

Today's economy, with its ruthless competitors and unforgiving customers, demands more and more work from employees in companies well beyond the start-up stage. In spite of time-saving technology, people today are working as long and as hard as did our forefathers, maybe more. It is still sunup to sundown, with work on the home computer or laptop following a long day at the shop. And unfortunately, going to work on the weekends is increasingly being required, or is seen as the only time anyone can get anything done without being constantly interrupted.

There are two other compounding factors that shed some light on the dominance of work in our lives. Neither factors are helpful in the least. The first is our refusal to be satisfied. It's a cultural expectation: "Don't ever become satisfied!" We are forever bombarded by new and better conveniences, new and better makes and models, newer, safer, more comfortable neighborhoods, new and better toys and gadgets, and new and more exotic foods, drinks, and destinations. The marketers of consumerism would have us believe that to be satisfied with who you are and what you already have is tantamount to giving up on getting ahead. Never being satisfied translates into, "Your family isn't as important as the things you surround them with."

The other factor in the dominance of work in our lives is more insidious. Many people have little capacity for closeness. They grew up in families where intimacy was neither provided nor role modeled. This is reflected and reinforced in our entertainment. Movies, television, and music, especially country-western music with all its broken hearts, being left behind, traveling the lonely road again, and sleeping single in a double bed, reveal a culture that is uneasy with loving relationships, and their cradle, home life. We end up a culture that finds safety in work. It is easier to work than it is to build family relationships, especially close, caring, honest, and abiding relationships.

## Family Neglect Is News

The dominance of work takes a devastating toll on our family lives. So much so that even business literature has been addressing the issue. Consider the titles and subtitles of *Fortune* magazine articles:

"Can Your Career Hurt Your Kids?" Mommy often gets home from work too tired to talk. Daddy's almost never around. Says one expert: "We can only guess at the damage being done to the very young." (May 20, 1991)

"Is Your Family Wrecking Your Career? (And Vice Versa?)" The dirty little secret is this: For all its politically correct talk, your company doesn't much like your kids. (March 17, 1997)

"The Myth of Quality Time." Kids don't do meetings. You can't raise them in short, scheduled bursts. They need lots of attention, and experts warn that working parents may be shortchanging them. (May 12, 1997)

These titles aren't from some so-called touchy-feely social, religious, psychological brochure passed out at some weekend marriage enrichment workshop. They are from the creators of the Fortune 500! We have come that far with our deification of work. The Nazis, however, were still wrong when they purported: *Arbeiten Macht Frei* (work makes free, literally). Work doesn't make anyone free if it is basically the only activity in life.

## THE PRICE PAID

It is in this work/success pressure cooker that family businesses try to combine work and family. They are to be admired. Their effort to work with each other day in and day out is downright valiant. By no stretch of the imagination could this possibly be easy. It is much easier, of course, to cheat the family side of the equation, and allow the business side to take over the heart of the family's attention and energies. It is inevitable, then, that sooner or later virtually every family member wonders, "What could be more important than our family?"

This longing question is especially poignant to those who have experienced the pressure:

> *It turns out I am not with my kids as much as I'd like to be or should be. It hurts when my daughter says on the phone, "Will you tuck me in tonight?" and I'm clear across the country on a business trip.*
>
> Mike, age thirty-nine, CEO,
> son of founder, construction company

*The worst time of the day is when I say good-bye at the day care center. He clings so tight, crying because he's been there twelve hours every day this week so far. I'm a wreck before I even get to our office. And at night we're all exhausted. We're missing too much. I'm beginning to feel it's not worth it.*

Collette, age forty, physician
in practice with physician husband

*Sure I love being a grandfather. But you know, my daughter's already back here at work just two months after the little guy's birth. Grandma loves taking care of him and his older brother. But my daughter's missing out on so much. She's not really back in the old groove around here yet. But what would I do without her working here? She's my best employee.*

Elton, age seventy-one, semiretired
founder of agriculture chemical company

*My father never, no not once, said he loved me. I know he did, sort of, in his own way. But he could have said it just once, damn him. He died and I never told him I loved him either. On his death bed he told me to keep my head down during my golf swing. That's as close as he could get to telling me he cared. And we worked together everyday since I was a teenager. I love him and hate him to this day.*

Bill, age forty-four, owner,
restaurant chain

*We weren't what you'd call a family. Our parents were never happy with each other. So dad married the business and mom married us kids. And then he'd come home and try to run the family like he ran the business. My older brother knuckled under. That's why he's president of the company now. The rest of us didn't count—we weren't valuable to the business because we had other interests. So we weren't valuable to dad either.*

Angela, age thirty-nine, teacher,
one-third owner, tool and die company

*When I married into this family I had no clue their family business would swallow us up. We even have to live on the farm property. They gave the land and the house to us free. Free meant we had no other choice. You can't do anything without them knowing it, and without passing judgment. We have no life. It's just the family farm 365 days a year. And when my husband tries to cut his hours, or go somewhere with me, especially if it's away for a couple of days, you should hear them badmouth me to him, or sarcastically tease him about not being the man of the house.*

Jackie, age twenty-eight, homemaker,
family dairy farm

*I don't give a damn about my brothers and one sister. All they want is their annual dividend check. All the while begrudging me mine, as though somehow my salary for working here is all I should get. I'm the one supporting all of them. Our parents love us all, and want desperately to treat us all equally. But there's no love lost between us kids. I want to buy them all out someday, even at the exorbitant prices they're dreaming of. It'd be worth it. They're just freeloading off mom and dad anyway. And off me too.*

Scott, age forty-seven, president/CEO,
food processing company

*It was amazing at dad's funeral. All the honors he received over the years. All his friends from work, all the dignitaries from the community, all his golfing and fishing cronies, the guest clergy from out of town. We just sat there. It was like we never knew him. We wish he had talked more. He never let his family in. Oh, he was good to us and all that. It's just that he was this kindly stranger who loved others more than he loved us.*

Allan, age fifty-one, controller,
sheet metal contractor

These lamentations are the harvest of seeds sown in the springtime of most family businesses. Decisions were made early on to sacrifice all for the sake of the business's survival. The sacrifice worked, so more was called for to guarantee the business's continued success. The business mattered most. Simultaneously, the marriage of the founder went through the normal seasons, the children grew through their normal developmental stages, and the extended family matured through its life cycles. All this family history flew past as a blur, because it was not at the focus of attention. The family's business mattered most. The family paid the price—home life neglected.

## YEARNING FOR HOME LIFE

When everything is sacrificed to the point of neglecting the family, there is always a yearning for home life:

- A yearning for affection and caring beyond the substitute gifts and opportunities, however well-meaning
- A yearning for special attention by every member of the family, because every family member wants to be cherished as an individual, not just for being a mere family member
- A yearning for closeness, so that things of the heart can be sorted out with someone who deeply cares
- A yearning to escape loneliness, our most painful emotion
- A yearning for making peace with each other before it is too late, even if it is merely a clumsy apology and a shy word of forgiveness

All this is quietly, and at times not so quietly, going on behind the scenes of a family overworking a business and undergrowing a family at the same time.

## SUMMARY

Family life, like the business, is a responsibility. Although family life has its wonderful privileges, it is not really a privilege itself. Its rewards are not possible without the necessary input. It requires a level of commitment, passion, courage, and loyalty that business success requires. Those who value family life are constantly guided by the question, "What's best for our family?" They ask this question and allow it to guide their priorities.

Instinctively everyone knows that Andre Malraux strikes a chord when he observed,

> A friend loves you for your intelligence, a mistress for your charm; but your family's love is unreasoning: You were born into it and of its flesh and blood. Without a family, man, alone in the world, trembles with the cold.

Or as Paul McCartney put it in his "Liverpool Oratorio":[1]

> What people want is a family life,
> The strength of a home and a moat round the castle.
> Pull up the drawbridge,
> Staying at home with the family.
>
> All people want is a family life.
> Sometimes they find it isn't so easy.
> People can argue.
> Life can be hard in a family.
>
> But people still want a family life.
> Nothing replaces the love and affection.
> Pull up the drawbridge . . . .

*Text from "Liverpool Oratorio" by Paul McCartney*
*Copyright © 1990 by MPL Communications Ltd.*
*Reproduced by permission of Faber Music Ltd.*

## BACK TO THE BASICS

Sit down with your immediate family members and take turns discussing the following:

1. Five of your favorite childhood memories.
2. The dream you had when you were younger about what kind of family you hoped to have someday.
3. Ten things you appreciate most about your family today.
4. A recent time you felt pangs of loneliness.
5. How your family could have one family night a week that would be good for everyone.

## CHAPTER SIX

# Marriage Best Practices

*We just celebrated our fiftieth wedding anniversary. It was real nice. All the kids and grandchildren were here. Friends came from all over. Even some of our longtime employees came to the party. The rest of them had a cake for us at the office. They called Doris without me knowing it. I guess the kids told them it was our golden anniversary. After we cut the cake, like a couple of newlyweds, they sang "Happy Anniversary" and shouted "speech, speech." You know how people do. So I told them, the secret to being married this long has been my wife's patience with me. That got a laugh. But it's no bull. Then I told them that Doris and I have been friends since high school, and that we never stopped being friends. That's the real secret, you know. Staying friends. We're enjoying life together like never before, now that I'm not working so much. The good Lord willing, hopefully we can have many more years together.*

> Joe, age seventy-one, semiretired
> founder, local telephone company

I HAVE NEVER MET ANYONE WHO DID NOT WANT WHAT is best for his or her family. Good intentions are always there, even though performance may be lacking. People marry, have children, become grandparents, and leave gifts after death all with the best of intentions. And yet, most family businesses I have worked with have claimed that family matters can too easily trip them up. It is family matters that have the most potential to ruin their businesses, in spite of good intentions. I have heard so often what has become a refrain in family business consulting: "Running the business is the easy part. It's the family end of things that really get to us."

Virtually every single family business consulting assignment I have had over the past two decades has involved family relationship issues, either up front, or eventually. These difficulties could have been either partially prevented or very much reduced had families had a better understanding of what is involved in the complexities of family life. Their understanding of what is involved in making a business tick surpasses their understanding of what makes a family tick.

## FAMILY MATTERS MOST

It is not surprising that most all of us are more knowledgeable about how to grow a business than we are about how to nurture a family. No small reason for this is the fact that family life is infinitely more complicated than the business world. It is more difficult to understand, let alone succeed in. Business yields more easily to rationality (although it is far more emotional that business people like to admit). Family life, by contrast, does not easily yield to rationality, although at times being rational is called for. Rather, family life is so much more encompassing. It defies easy discussion because it embraces things that only the arts, especially music, drama, comedy, and religion (which also relies on the arts), can touch. Nonetheless, there are families in every culture and in every age that have intuitively figured out how to make their home life successful. They have created family best practices, just as successful businesses have invented business best practices. They have done so because they wanted to practice what they believed—family matters a great deal to them.

These chapters on family best practices will seem unusual to readers of business literature. The people side of business only gets passing mention in the best of business reading. Fuller discussions of family matters in family business literature are rare. But families in family business not only live out these issues everyday, both at home and at work, but also value common sense consultation on the very things that matter most to them. Family *matters* in family business, beginning with the most important *matter* of all, the marriage.

## HUSBANDS AND WIVES

There is fundamentally nothing so vital to families than the quality of the parents' marriage. This cannot be exaggerated. The marriage is the heart of the family. As the marriage goes, so goes the family. It is the defining relationship. It determines the physical and emotional health of the spouses and even more powerfully of the children. Children desperately want their parents to love each other and be good to and for each other. This is true whether the children are young, are teenagers, or are grown adults. I have never worked with a struggling youngster, a troubled adolescent, a substance abusing adolescent or adult, or a suicidal person of any age, whose parents had a good marriage. Usually one or both spouses going through emotional or legal divorce have parents whose marriages were wanting.

Success with marriage has never been more complicated than it is today. This owes to the expectations couples now bring to marriage. They are looking for deep emotional fulfillment. Yesterday's motivations have very little influence. People do not marry for economic, religious, sexual, or romantic reasons. Some do not marry even to have children. Marriage as simply a tradition—everyone does it because it is expected by a certain age—is no more. Rather, couples start with what has always made for the best of marriages—friendship, that is, deep friendship, complete friendship, and lasting friendship that is emotionally fulfilling. Today's couples do not want to just settle for love. They place a highest premium on liking each other. They want to like each other, and be liked by the other, as they never before have experienced a friendship. They saw their parents probably love each other, but not *like* each other very much.

Couples today want to belong to each other as best friends. They want to be thoroughly understood and accepted. They want to be supported and encouraged in their individual fulfillment. As much as they want a meaningful friendship, today's couples are very much part of today's culture of individualism. They expect their friendship-based marriages to support and enhance their individual pursuits. But they do not want to be lonely in these individual endeavors. They want a friend who will not abandon them. They want someone who will bring out the best in them, cheering them on from the sidelines. They want someone with whom mutual pleasures can be enjoyed.

The irony in all this is how frequently couples unwittingly assume that their quest for deep emotional fulfillment will naturally, even magically, be successful once they have said their vows. In this they are probably no different than their parents or grandparents. Of course, nothing could be more romantically naive. They want so earnestly for their marriage to succeed, but they forget what is needed "from this day forward." Here is a reminder list of seven of the most basic marriage best practices.

## MARRIAGE BEST PRACTICES

### The All-Determining Decision

Well-married spouses make a decision to be well-married. Theirs is an individual decision and a mutual decision. This is not the same as deciding to get married. It is a deep down decision to be your spouse's deepest, most trustworthy friend. Too many married people never have decided to be truly married. Not making this deep commitment is to assume that some sort of cruise control is good enough to power a young relationship. Not to decide is to end up automatically with a photocopy of one's parents' marriage. Not to decide is to allow outsiders, whether parents, in-laws, siblings, friends or work colleagues, to unduly influence the marriage. This decision to be well-married includes the following commitments, which in turn means honest, continuous effort:

- To make this relationship the highest of priorities
- To build each other up, rather than criticize, correct, and complain about each other
- To be emotionally open with each other, rather than remain strangers by covering up important, deeper parts of oneself
- To accept each other, rather than futilely try to change each other
- To protect each other from loneliness
- To cheer each other's growth and successes, rather than jealously keep the other person down
- To accommodate each other's differences, and benefit from them, rather than condemn the inevitable differences as wrong
- To agree to disagree, rather than treat disagreement as reason for rejection, or reason for shrill intolerance
- To discuss and resolve differences as they occur, rather than allow them to pile up by sweeping them under the rug
- To spend some time just with each other, rather than always double-dating with children, relatives, work associates, and friends

The decision from the heart and mind to be each other's best friend means that neither person will do anything that would fundamentally hurt the foundation on which the relationship is built. There will be umpteen bumps in the road, of course, and bolts out of the blue, and butting of heads. There will be many temptations to be unfaithful, especially the temptations to marry the children, marry the family business, marry church or society activities, marry sports and recreation, or get tangled up with another potential "best" friend, either emotionally or physically. But the decision to be well-married means that no action or outside relationship will be allowed to threaten the foundation commitment to each other to be emotionally fulfilling best friends.

## Mutual Trust and Mutual Respect

The second best practice of marriage is spouses treating each other with mutual trust and mutual respect. No relationship can function without these twin qualities, whether at work or at home. Nothing lasting can be built between people if they cannot count on each other—trust—and if they are not careful with what is important to the other—respect.

Trust means couples can count on each other. Trust is behavior, not words. Trust has to be proved. Trust is usually partially given and earned during the first few dates. Then it is earned in repeated ways during courtship. At marriage, trust is normally given completely— couples assuming they will be able to count on each other forever. From the wedding on, trust has to be continuously reinforced. If, however, trust is slightly violated, doubts will plague the relationship. If massively violated, trust is seldom fully re-earned—it silently accompanies the couple as suspicion—something to be continuously lived down.

Couples who trust each other behave in ways that translate as follows:

> You can count on me and I will count on you. I won't let you down, and I am counting on not being let down by you. I am more for us than I am simply out for myself. I'm counting on the same from you. I won't do anything that will erode or violate the foundation of our relationship. You can count on me with other people, with our money, with my health and safety, and with my priorities. I want to count on you in the same ways. To me our relationship is sacred, and I am counting on you to regard us as sacred too.

Respect means couples are careful with what is of importance to the other. A partial list of what is important to both spouses almost always includes each other's ideas, feelings, hopes and dreams, time, health, sex, extended family, nonfamily relationships, and values. For example, if the wife's ideas and opinions are not taken into consider- ation, she will not feel respected. If the husband's feelings are not drawn out and listened to with understanding, he will not feel respected. If the wife is repeatedly left waiting for her always-late and procrastinating husband, she will feel her time violated by his disrespect. If the husband's professional or recreational dreams are denigrated, he will not feel respected. If the wife's career goals, whether inside or outside the home, are treated as secondary to whatever the husband does, she will not feel herself respected as an equal in the relationship. If the husband's attempts at parenting are belittled, he will not feel fatherhood is as respected as motherhood in his own home. If the wife's need to feel close before making love is disregarded, she will feel used and disrespected. If either's relationship to their background families is discounted in importance, there will be the feeling of disrespect.

Intimate friends committed to each other's emotional fulfillment are simply very caring and very careful with what is vital to the other. It is the way to show respect.

## Friendly Separation from Parents

The third best practice of solid marriages is achieving a friendly separation from parents. This is a difficult challenge for families working together in their own businesses. Too often married couples lose their marital identity by getting swallowed up, not just by the business, but by the extended family that comes with it. Unless a married couple separates in friendly ways from their parents, they will struggle to grow up. And they will struggle to grow closer to each other as a unique, autonomous couple writing its own history. They end up not standing on their own four feet.

To separate from in-laws, couples need the privacy that geography can provide, at least living across town from both sets of parents. They need the discipline of having their own earned budget. They need the freedom from parental interference in order to create their own ways of doing things. Couples need to develop their own tools of communication, accommodating, negotiating, and experimenting—the very skills needed at every stage in the future. Shortcutting this maturing process by going to mom and dad, or allowing mom and dad to interfere, no matter how well meaning their intentions, cheats the couple from maturing as friends who seek deep emotional fulfillment from each other.

On a deeper level, parting from one's parents is an emotional necessity for growing up. Even couples who are self-supporting and do not run to or invite in-laws to rescue them, have to work hard at not simply reliving their childhood homes. There is the seemingly automatic tendency to treat one's spouse not the way the couple decides, but the way their parents related as spouses. A mask of mother or father is seen on the face of the spouse with behavior in response resembling childish rebellion or compliance. No wonder all those exasperated judgments: "You're just like your old lady," with the rejoinder, "Yeh, but you treat me as though I were your mother. Besides, you're your father, through and through." Volumes have been written about psychological maturity, which suggests the process is incredibly complex, and there is no one way to achieve it. Suffice it to say here, becoming your own couple begins with the decisions to be well-married, to grow up with each other, and to resist the temptation of copying one's parents.

Another point about friendly separation from one's parents. It is about the word *friendly*. Parents and in-laws deserve some slack. Actually, forgiveness. They are all too human, just as we all are. They were young and struggling as individuals, as a couple, and as bread-winners when they had the most influence on their children. They said a lot of things they did not mean, a lot of things they only meant rhetorically, and things they in fact did mean, but not with the force remembered by children. They deserve some generous slack for all this. All parents deserve to be forgiven for being young when they had children. More likely than not they were doing their best with what they knew, in the circumstances they had.

Seen in this light, parents deserve a friendly parting from their adult children. This involves the couple carrying on what was good about their backgrounds, and improving on what was not. It includes making the best of the times when everyone is together. This usually means sticking to topics of the here and now, and doing enjoyable things together, rather than bringing up the old stink bombs of yesterday. Intergenerational enjoyment is very crucial, especially for grandchildren. And positive humor is one of the most important ingredients of a good relationship between parents, in-laws, and grown children. Humor, after all, is the shortest distance between people, as Victor Borge once said. And many good, fun, easy-going times together can pave the way for the time when it is necessary to resolve old hurts and issues. Sabotaging every family gathering with bad stuff of the past is a sure sign that either the parents do not see their children as grown-ups, or the adult children are refusing to grow up and get their own show on the road.

One last point. Parents are parents until they die. They always worry about their kids and always want to help, whether it is advice or money, whether their children are twenty-one years old or seventy-one years old. Like the elderly mother in a retirement home telling her pastor how worried she was that her son was unemployed. As she went on, it finally dawned on the pastor to ask her age: "I'm ninety-one and my son is seventy-one. He needs to be working."

Regarding advice, parents are not always wrong. Sometimes it may be a good idea to take their advice, even if they want you to. Regarding money, it is best not to ask for it. When money is offered as a judicious assist, or a gift of shared fortune, rather than as a rescue or dependency-creating move, it may be a good idea to accept their generosity. Parents genuinely enjoy helping their kids no matter their age—their children will always be kids to them. A friendly parting from one's parents makes it possible over time for parents to respect the sanctity of their children's adult marriage.

## Time for Pleasure

The fourth best practice of marriage is time management for pleasure. Most couples are adept at managing their time for responsibilities. Somehow, time is found for work, daily and weekly chores, some parenting, some exercise, some individual recreation, some socializing, some continuing education, some religious and community service, some extended family events, and some sleep. But the very thing that worked so well in bonding the couple together in the first place, the pleasure of each other's company, is given the leftovers of time. Usually nothing is left over.

Early in relationships, couples find time for each other. They fall in love by talking and listening to each other for hours, even on the phone, no matter the cost in time or money. Perhaps for the first time in their lives they find pleasure in talking and listening. They go on walks, have leisurely dinners out, share favorite music, nominate some songs as their songs, enjoy deliciously long explorations of each other physically, invent their own jokes and lingo, divulge deep dark secrets to each other, especially about their parents and siblings, go on pleasure jaunts out of town, and create a nonverbal affection repertoire they use constantly. For the first time since early childhood they reexperience the benefits of pleasure that become avenues of endearment. All this underscores how we humans are pleasure-seeking beings: the brain is programmed to avoid danger and pain, and is loaded with pleasure centers that can repeatedly give wings to the heart. Part of the implicit contract of marriage is to live together pleasurably—to experience pleasure with each other. Home turns out to be not like the outside world, but a nice, safe, comfortable refuge of pleasure, away from the outside world.

This requires time management. And time management sounds like work! It is, especially for couples committed to success at work and success at home at the same time. Time management for married pleasure thus requires the discipline to set aside time for all the things that originally paved the way for closeness. This is not to say that spontaneity has no place in marriage. But most couples do not even give spontaneity a chance. Time for it has to be shoehorned into a hectic schedule of responsibility. It does seem artificial to put a dynamic relationship on some schedule. But what is the alternative? Leaving marital pleasure to chance? Fat chance it will happen. If it is not put on the calendar, it simply will not happen. If it is not decided on together, it will not happen. If it is not planned for, it will not happen. The couple then will be on the slippery slope to becoming strangers to each other.

What couples do with their time is always a matter of choice. They can choose to withdraw from each other, go through the motions together, do activities alone, work together or alone, fight together (and sometimes this is done alone too), or seek pleasure with each other. All time management is decision-making about what is important. Well-married couples have pleasure as a priority. So at the risk of offering a cookiecutter formula, I encourage couples to at least follow the minimums, which unfortunately is more than most neglected relationships ever get:

- Talk and listen daily for thirty minutes
- Call everyday when you are out of town
- Plan your weekends every Wednesday evening
- Have at least four hours of pleasure planned for just the two of you two weekends a month
- Do not allow double dating and extended family events to substitute for your time alone together
- Each spouse initiate sex weekly
- Enjoy an overnight out of town, or a weekend night at home, without the children, on a quarterly basis
- Have at least a four-day honeymoon annually (no guests allowed)

Well-married couples do not look back and sigh, "We always got everything done. Too bad we didn't enjoy it. It's been all beans and no ice cream, all marches and no dancing, all midnight oil and no moonlight. If only we had it to do over again . . ."

## Value Your Differences

A fifth marriage best practice is spouses allowing themselves to be positively influenced by each other's differences. There is the overwhelming tendency to marry someone opposite in temperament and demeanor. Opposites attract. While it is true that couples are attracted to each other because of all the things they share in common, like interests, tastes, backgrounds, education, intelligence levels, values, and worldview, it is just as true that the differences are even more compelling. It is the old Jack Spratt principle: "Jack Spratt could eat no fat. His wife could eat no lean. But together they licked the platter clean."

Opposites do attract. One is hot, the other cool. One is outgoing, the other reserved. One is impulsive, the other cautious. One is blunt, the other gentle. One is a dreamer, the other is practical. One is organized and efficient, the other is casual and slow paced. One shows love by doing and fixing (usually the man), the other shows love by relating and taking care of (usually the woman). One wants to solve things (usually the man), the other wants to talk things through (usually the woman). One wants to be playful and goof around (usually the man), the other wants to seriously relate first (usually the woman). One wants sex in order to feel good (usually the man), the other wants to have sex when things are good (usually the woman). One is seldom satisfied (usually the man), the other wants the relationship to be satisfying first (usually the woman).

This attraction of opposites comes from two sources. One is that likes repel. Two people with a lot of heat would have a torrid weekend, but end up throwing china by Sunday evening. Two reserved people would die of boredom. Two talkers would not have anyone listening. If both waited until everything were perfect before having sex, they would have sex once every other leap year, whether they needed it or not.

The other reason opposites attract is the need each spouse has to be more complete. An impulsive person needs the limits and self-control of the other. The cautious person needs some pizzazz and salsa in his or her life. A blunt person needs the softening tenderness of the other. A softie needs some backbone and what it takes to enforce limits—qualities the other has.

Well-married couples realize that these differences in temperament and demeanor are the tinder for many marital brush fires. Oppositeness has to be treated carefully, lest the strengths of each become the spark to inflame the relationship. But if couples appreciate how their differences are as much the glue of their marriage as are their mutual trust, mutual respect, and mutual pleasures, they will allow themselves to be positively influenced and balanced by each other. They will be open to maturing, with the help of the other's example and input. Rather than being intolerant or dismissive of the other's best qualities, they will partially incorporate the other's differences. After years of careful push and pull, a well-married person will be able to say, "I'm a better person because my best friend brought out the best in me, and loaned me her strength when I didn't have it myself."

## Caring, Not Taking Care Of

Well-married couples mutually care for each other. They do not necessarily take care of each other as a matter of course. One is not the full-time caretaker, or caregiver, while the other is always on the receiving end. Couples who care for each other do a good job of balancing the giving and receiving of each other's care. They do this by listening, encouraging, supporting, and defending each other. They are grown-ups who respect the strengths, capabilities and potential of the other. They are equal partners. They are adults to each other. They are not parent and child to each other, with one spouse parenting the other day in and day out.

Couples who have a parent/child relationship have a dominating spouse who knows best, makes all the decisions, calls all the shots, and is generally in charge. The recipient of this parenting is either passive, needy, careless, or demanding, like a two year old who has to have what he wants, when he wants it, or else he will throw a fit. This is the worst case of opposites attracting—one wants to baby someone, and the other wants to be babied.

The most common example of this is the big momma/little boy relationship, where the husband, although quite capable and responsible at work, plays helpless and demanding at home. He expects to be waited on hand and foot. He did his part for family life: he worked all day outside the home. Home to him, like it is to children, is hotel living, where management (read wife) caters in hope of a tip—that is, a pleasant and quiet guest. The wife comes by all this quite honestly. Women commendably accept responsibility for the emotional and comfort womb of family life, ending up unfortunately giving and giving and giving without much appreciation or reward. The husband ends up as the oldest and biggest kid in the family. But the wife is responsible for some of this as well. It is not uncommon for wives to disempower their husbands as equally important partners, shoving the husband aside when he finally does try to be a grown-up in the family.

The other common example is big daddy/little girl. Here it is the husband who is all knowing, all wise, all helpful, all controlling. He is convinced his wife needs to be taken care of. He parents her as her teacher, guidance counselor, provider, and protector. The wife plays into this with false naiveté, low self-confidence, and dependency on her husband's decision making.

These marriages are prescriptions for loneliness and trouble. Adult closeness, mutual sexuality, equality of give and take, and the joys of shared responsibility are absent. Distance, resentment, and arrested maturity drive the couple apart. In family businesses where there is a big momma/little boy relationship at home, the wife will come to resent the business, where the husband is a responsible performer and admired as being a great guy. This is not how he is at home. In the big daddy/little girl relationship, the husband will come to resent the demands of home life and the neediness of his wife, who is so different from the capable, attractive women at work.

Well-married couples avoid these imbalances of giving and receiving. Over the long haul they feel that each has given and received equally. They realize there will be times, such as illness, business downturns, busy seasons, and caretaking demands of elderly parents, for example, when the need to give more than one receives is understandable. But even in these times, well-married couples know that they equally care for each other as adults, and that neither is a little kid who has to be taken care of. They appreciate, too, that over the long haul, giving and receiving will balance out. They are confident of this, because they care for each other as grownup friends.

## Flexibility

Well-married people practice flexibility. They have learned to be flexible people because they found out that rigidity is the path to loneliness. They have seen how devastating rigidity can be, having seen it in their background families, extended families, and school and work experiences.

Rigidity takes the form of:

- Having to always be right
- Having to have everything perfect
- Having to be controlling, and have everything in control
- Having to be constantly liked
- Having to have everything harmonious
- Having to slug everything out right now
- Having to be agreed with, or else
- Having everyone be religiously, socially, politically, psychologically, or gastronomically correct
- Having to point out the negative, no matter how much it is outweighed by the positive
- Having nothing emotional, or tender, or needy expressed
- Having to always work before play
- Allowing no one else to be happy if it has been a bad day
- Having to borrow tomorrow's possible problems for today's worry, so today cannot be possibly good for anyone
- Having to exaggerate the negative, to the point of believing that catastrophe is knocking on the door right now

The list, unfortunately, could go on and on.

These rigidities make life hell for rigid persons and for everyone else around them. Rigid people would rather have things their way than be close to the people they claim to love. Well-married couples realize that family life requires flexible give and take by each spouse.

They realize that compromise is not weakness. They know that the Golden Rule—treat others as you want to be treated—begins in families with the husband and wife. They do not tolerate one person being the weather, while everyone else, especially the spouse, having to constantly adjust to the rigid person's highs and lows, like a passive barometer. Well-married people practice flexibility because the short term victories of rigidity are hollow compared to the long term benefits of closeness. A spouse who has decided to be a best friend frequently concedes . . .

- I'd rather be close, than right.

- I'd rather be close, than have everything my way.

- I'd rather be close, than pretending everything is just fine, when there are things that need to be discussed and resolved.

- I'd rather be close, than have everyone see things my way, as though our family has no freedom of thought or speech.

- I'd rather be close, than work myself into a dither with worry, driving everyone else around me nuts.

Closeness is worth the practice of flexibility.

## SUMMARY ON MARRIAGE BEST PRACTICES

Given how challenging a family business is to family life, each generation of owners needs and deserves solid marriages at home. Good marriages make for good families. Good families enhance the chances for success in their business. Family matters are developed and dealt with at home, not at work. As a result, family matters in family business do not interfere, subtract, or cripple the business. And this is much more likely to happen when husbands and wives in family businesses . . .

- Decide to be each other's deepest, most loyal friends
- Practice mutual trust and mutual respect
- Separate from their parents, in a friendly way, in order to be grown-ups in their own right
- Set aside time for the pleasure of each other's company
- Value each other's differences, allowing the other's oppositness to be a positive influence
- Care for each other as adults, rather than living a parent/child relationship
- Choose to be flexible, in order to experience closeness more often

## BACK TO THE BASICS

For couples only:

1. Go out on a dinner date and tell each other ten things you most appreciate and admire about the other, and ten positive things about your home life.
2. On another dinner date, tell each other what things you enjoyed most back when you were first got together; select one to do again, for old time's sake, getting the date on the calendar.
3. Begin using a half hour on Wednesday evenings to plan the upcoming weekend.
4. Take a long walk together and discuss one thing you each need from the other in order to feel closer.
5. Take another long walk and discuss how the two of you can better observe the boundary between home life and business.

## CHAPTER SEVEN

# Parenting Best Practices

*I have my secretary clear my calendar for all my daughter's swim meets, and for all my son's little league games. I won't miss one, because I had always wished my dad had come to all my games. He was always down here at the office. You know how he is—not much of a delegator. My sister works here too, as a part-timer, because of her two little ones. I'm glad we can work that out for her. She comes in late, and leaves early. Trouble is, none of the other women do. And I know they'd like to. We just don't know how to create a family-friendly company for everyone, and still get the job done and keep costs down. And we're a family business! I feel guilty about this. Our employees feel the same for their kids, as we do about ours. It doesn't help to complain about family life in America and do nothing about it.*

Rick, age thirty-six, president/CEO,
marketing/advertising agency

THERE IS NO MORE PROFOUNDLY POWERFUL ATTACH-ment in life than the attachment parents have to their children. It is impossible to exaggerate this. Parents are forever attached at the heart to their own flesh and blood. I am convinced parents unconditionally love their children more than they ever love anyone else. Including their own spouses. Almost every parent I have ever known would sacrifice everything they have, including their own lives, for the sake of their children. Most, however, would think twice before making any monumental sacrifice for their spouses, some even thinking twice before making a minor sacrifice!

Many parents go so far as tolerating their own unrewarding marriages for the sake of their children. They stay together as "gruesome twosomes," just to be some sort of a unified family for the kids' sakes, not realizing or admitting what a disservice this can be for the children. Even in divorced families parents commonly emerge as better parents than ever before. This is especially true of men who, for the first time, begin taking fatherhood seriously. So strong is nature's way with parents for their children.

Even parents who blew it while the kids were young, by being, for example, absent too much of the time, feel a surge of dedication to their children before it is too late. I suspect that is why some parents with family businesses make their kids the top executives and chief beneficiaries of the business, regardless of fit or merit. It is a belated act of love to make up for the years when their young business took precedence over their young children.

This deep, deep attachment parents feel for their children undoubtedly influenced Martin Luther, the former monk turned father of a brood of children, to guess that "God's love is like a mother bending over a dirty diaper."

Although parents do not want to be told how to raise their kids by relatives and friends, parents nonetheless have readily embraced parenting literature, and advice from pediatricians, family doctors, and child psychologists. Parenting best practices have thus become quite widely known. The five parenting best practices highlighted here are by no means the whole story. They are, however, widely accepted, based on common sense, and are part of what matters to families owning their own businesses.

## PARENTING BEST PRACTICES

### Enjoy Your Children

Why do you suppose babies are so darn cute when they smile? Why do they giggle when you blow bubbles under their arms, or when you play peek-a-boo with them? Why do preschoolers say the darndest things, have such outrageous imaginations, and love to play tricks on you? Why do school-age children still love to roughhouse with you, pretending they are so big, yet wait for you to say good night? Why are teenagers such fascinating, oh-so-carefully dressed, hyper-self-conscious people, who straight arm you at the very moment they are really wanting a hug? Why are young adults equally fascinating as they extend their adolescence to thirty years of age, going through potential partners, and trying out different jobs, to get it all just right? Why is it so intriguing to watch your children become parents in their own right, shifting into a super-charged-responsibility gear you never knew they had, becoming just as possessive with their children as you were with them? Why is it so amusing to see adult kids put on weight and lose hair, act, think, and look more and more like you, and even come around to finally appreciating you, their parent, as a real person?

Why? Because children are, first and foremost, enjoyable. As the old saying goes, "Children are the best evidence yet that God has a sense of humor." Children want nothing so much as to be the apple of your eye. No one outgrows the desire, yes, the need, to be looked upon approvingly and joyfully by parents: "Look, mom, no hands!" Children are to be enjoyed.

Almost all kids know their parents love them, even if parents do not demonstrate or articulate it very well. But more importantly, all kids want their parents to enjoy them. This is why parents continually hear from young children, "Play with me." This is why the big kid in the family, aka father, is so popular with the kids at bedtime when he winds them up with goof-off time. This is why kids do not want to do any chores when mom is home. They have not had a moment's worth of enjoyment with her for weeks, since she is too frequently inundated by work. This is why teenagers are crushed when their parents do not attend their athletic games or artistic recitals, even though they will not talk to you all the way to the event or on the way back home afterwards. This is why adult children in conversation with parents allow for pauses while discussing their own kids or careers, hoping, consciously and unconsciously, to hear how much their parents approve and admire how they are doing. This is why elderly parents want their children and grandchildren to call and visit more often. All this is in service of children wanting to be enjoyed by their parents. And vice versa later in life.

What does this have to do with family business? A lot. I applaud the many younger-generation owners who are cutting back on their hours to have more family time. Many are taking off from work to attend their kids' events. They bring their kids to work and introduce them around. They decorate their offices, not with stuffy institutional fare, but with all the whimsical artwork of their kids, let alone photographs galore. Time and again these younger family business owners have told me,

*I'm not going to make the same mistake dad did. We never saw him when we were kids. And he missed out on so much. It was a big loss to him, as it was to us. My kids are too important. I can see what my parents now mean when they say to enjoy the kids now because they grow up so fast.*

Mike, age thirty-nine, founder's son,
president/CEO of a construction company

I also think it is crucial to reserve some part of family time for enjoyment. This is important for an individual family and for extended families in business together as well. I have worked with too many families who have come to dread family gatherings, because business talk and business relationships dragged home from work sap the spirit of the family.

*All they ever talk about is farming, unless of course there's a football game to watch. Some of the gossip from work is interesting, but the rest of it gets sickening. It's like they're still at work. I know most of us would like to just relax. And for those of us not at the company, we're left out. They don't feel we're very important—if you're not in, you don't count. You know what it is? It's that we don't know what else to talk about, or what else to do. We ought to just go outside and play with the kids, and forget the business. Sooner or later we will all be making excuses to skip the holidays and birthdays together. But that would hurt my in-laws. What are you going to do?*

Jackie, age twenty-eight, homemaker,<br>family dairy farm

A family's spirit comes from caring and enjoyment. Not shop talk.

It is too trite to say that the family that plays together stays together. But there are successful families owning successful businesses who have outlawed shop talk at all family gatherings in order to have more enjoyment together. They claim these enjoyable experiences bring them back together, enable them to be more patient with each other, and give them courage to address harder issues later on.

*Maybe the only time of the year we feel close as a family is when we go on our annual ski vacation. We all go, babies included. For once dad forgets the business and plays with the grandchildren like we wished he had played with us. Mom for once isn't excluded. And we switch off taking care of each other's kids. We get time alone as couples, and the kids have a ball. It's the only time of the year we don't have discipline problems with the kids. They thrive when we're all having fun together.*

Maria, age thirty-six, vice president,<br>family-owned winery

*I'm the one in the family who speaks up. And I knew there were bad feelings from work, and that Thanksgiving would be the*

*wrong time to bring that stuff up. And it was our turn to have everyone over to our house. So we literally dragged everyone to the neighborhood school yard. The kids didn't know grandma could skip rope, or that she was the champ of her fifth-grade class. Grandpa, Mr. Navy Blue Suit Himself, slipped in the mud for a big laugh. And my four-year-old niece ran the ball in for a touchdown. My brothers laughed with each other for the first time in months. You should hear the plans we have for Christmas. I'm not the only one, after all, who's sick of being so businesslike all the time.*

Todd, age forty-one, CPA,<br>family-owned accountancy firm

*The best thing we do all year is go duck hunting up north. Just me and the boys. I have no daughters. We even have our guns loaded! Things aren't very enjoyable at work at times, but when we're up there we let our hair down. I don't boss them around. We play cards, tell lies, and all that other b.s. And the only time we talk business is on the way back. The pictures we take and keep in the office tide us over when we're back in the thick of it.*

Buck, age sixty-six, owner,<br>diversified farming operation

Families who appreciate how vital enjoyment is to children observe an unwritten code when they get together: "We're here to enjoy ourselves. Don't bring up anything to mess this up. We're here to relax and enjoy our children."

Families that add enjoyment to their gatherings might have an easier time permitting some fun back at the business. This would do all the Type A's some good—they would not have to continue living in dread fear that someone, somewhere is having fun at work—they would be having just a little themselves. Enjoyment gives wings to the heart, shock absorbers to the personality, and springboards to courage. Besides, children are to be enjoyed.

## Tell Important Stories

Children love stories. Even in homes with too much TV watching, young children still beg, "Read to me, Mommy," or "Tell me that story again" for the thousandth time. Why do children love stories told and read by their parents? One reason is that children need, and indeed crave, the physical closeness and special attention that comes with storytelling. That would be reason enough to have story time a "routine" event, even though to a child, stories are never routine.

There is another equally important reason to tell stories. Children cannot distinguish between their inner and outer worlds until well along in their grammar-school training. As a result, they not only really get into stories, but they also incorporate into their hearts and minds the "truths" they hear in the stories. To put it another way, stories shape children's inner lives. Stories teach, like nothing else can.

This leads to storytelling as a parenting best practice of the first order. There are many important stories children revel in hearing, stories they also need to know. First among important stories is the story of your child's birth, emphasizing how much the child was wanted. To a child, this is the most important story of all. Kids, of course, enjoy all the anecdotes surrounding their birth: the who, where, when, and how of it all. But it is the why of it that is compelling. Children need to know that they were wanted. So tell them, again and again. They will never tire of this, their story. This is true for adopted children as well. Maybe more so. They need to hear that their natural mother wanted them to have a better life, and that their adopted parents genuinely wanted them. This story eases the inevitable pain of the perceived rejection by natural parents that most adopted children eventually struggle with, usually in early adolescence.

Another type of story children want to hear is family folklore. They love finding out about all the characters of your, and their own background. Children want to know whom they belong to. And they want to know how you size up these important and sometimes colorful people. Besides finding out what things are funny and amusing, children find out what can happen in life, how life can be handled, what you value, what life-influencing decisions you have made, and from what and whom you draw strength. Children pay attention to these stories.

Also tell your child stories where good triumphs over evil. These can include classic, epic stories of history and religion, as well as made-up stories about good kids and naughty kids, temptations resisted, bigotry overcome, loneliness befriended, and so on. Children can develop a deep, unconscious reservoir of strength, values, courage, and perseverance from these important stories. It is said that during the Holocaust it was the Orthodox Jews and Jehovah's Witnesses who demonstrated the greatest amounts of perseverance and survivability while interned in concentration camps. These two groups are noted for teaching their children from an early age on through adolescence the biblical epics of good versus evil.

Children listen intently also to stories of your own hard times, and how you handled them. This can come in bits and pieces over time as they become better able to handle your experiences. But they need to be introduced to some of life's realities and will learn what you learned and did not learn from your struggles. They also will feel closer to you as a result—their capacity for empathy reinforced for future relationships.

Families owning businesses have particularly important stories for their children and grandchildren. They need to learn about opportunity, risk taking, hard work, success, luck, hardships, mistakes, failures, responsibility, rewards, values, and perseverance. Every family business has a hundred stories about the people who founded it, the technology and products back then and now, the heroes and the goats, the changing customers and employees, the failures and successes. From all this, they will learn, most importantly, what it takes to succeed. They will take permission to succeed themselves. They can learn that the family business is a responsibility, a wonderful one at that, and not a privilege to which they are entitled.

Family matters in family business. So it matters that children born into these special families are nurtured, from childhood on through adulthood, by family storytelling. Tribal storytelling has been the mark of humans from the beginning of time. We can ill afford to be the generation that loses the art of telling our children stories they need to hear.

## Minimize Sibling Rivalry

If I were asked which two family matters are the most troubling to families in family business, I would say, "Number one is treating the business as a privilege, rather than as a responsibility. And number two is sibling rivalry." Sibling rivalry is never very far from the surface when brothers and sisters have to do business with each other.

Sibling rivalry is our tragic legacy. It is so much a part of family life that the Judeo-Christian Bible as early as page three, as part of the story, "In the Beginning," includes the tragedy of Cain and Abel. Soon thereafter come the stories of the brothers, Jacob and Esau, and of Joseph and his brothers, and later on, the prodigal son and his hardworking older brother. These ancient stories, unfortunately, have nothing over family businesses.

I know of two brothers who have not talked to each for close to thirty years now, because of a disagreement at the business they cofounded, a disagreement neither brother can remember very clearly. I have had to do shuttle diplomacy and mediation between siblings before we could even begin a strategic-planning retreat. And I know of a brother-in-law who quit the family business when he was passed over for the presidency, vowing along with his wife to never be part of the family again.

I know of two brothers whose relationship at work deteriorated to the point that verbal threats became reality, with a fistfight breaking out inside the office building, spilling out into the parking lot of the company in front of God and all the employees. I have seen siblings outside the family business begrudge the salaries of those siblings working inside the business. Their salaries were in fact lower than the average going rate in the area for positions of comparable responsibility and performance. I have seen a nonproductive sibling play on parental sentiment by borrowing obscene amounts of money for his own wild, unrealistic entrepreneurial fantasies that no bank would touch, only to fritter the money away on a lavish lifestyle—all in service of jealousy, because he never could be the star of the family business.

I have seen again and again founders who have "adopted" an outside young man or woman working within the company, and made this young person essentially a favored child. This lucky young person is usually someone more in the mold of the founder than his or her own sons and daughters. This outsider becomes an insider, receiving more attention, praise, and influence within the company than do the children. This adoption may make sense for the business, but it is seldom ever accepted by the founder's children without feelings of sibling rivalry. Their jealousy is not over the business sense of the outsider's rise in the organization. It is the parent's affection and pride for the outsider that is galling and resented.

And I have seen too many children try to fit into the family business just to finally be valued as a person in his or her own family. They vainly try to make their square peg fit into the round hole of the family business. It almost never pans out over the long haul, for the desperate child, for the family as a whole, and for the business. This losing situation happens because the parents are perceived as overvaluing contributions to the family's business. Those brothers and sisters who are business-minded are in the in-crowd as most favored children. Those with little or no aptitude for business feel like least favored children. Rather than hide or disappear from the family, the outsiders try to be something they are not. The dismal results unfortunately confirm the children's suspicions, their sibling rivalry reinforced for good.

In spite of this tragic legacy, however, sibling rivalry should not be something condemned out of hand. It cannot be "legislated" into extinction. It is a given, a given of the human condition, experienced by every family having more than one child. Every child born since Cain and Abel has wanted to be an only child. Deep in the soul of every person is the longing to be prized by one's parents as a unique, special person. Every kid wants to have exclusive rights to mom and dad. Having to share parents with others is traumatic and miserable in the beginning, and just tolerable later on.

Some parents, because of their own hang-ups, actually play favorites among their own children. Blatant favoritism is at the core of the Biblical stories cited above. And it is exposed for what it is—stupid. Fortunately, the vast majority of parents try their darndest to avoid favoring one child over the others. The trouble is, children find it easy to perceive favoritism anyway.

Favoritism is perceived when a younger child requires more time, attention, and work than older children. It can be perceived when one child is ill, or when one is cited for honors in school or sports. Favoritism is easily felt in large families where each child requires and expects their fair share of attention on a frequent basis. Perceived favoritism cannot be avoided in instant, new families, when stepbrothers and stepsisters have to suddenly share their own natural parents with these strangers. Family life is thus ripe for many inevitable, unintentional experiences of sibling rivalry.

The goal for parents is not to try to prevent sibling rivalry, or try to eradicate it from the family. Or what is even worse, parents should not deny it exists. The goal is to minimize sibling rivalry. Fortunately, there are some parenting best practices that can help.

The best thing parents can do to minimize sibling rivalry is to spend time privately with each child, no matter his or her age. And during that time, treat that child as though she or he were your only child, giving her or him your fullest attention. It would be best if you listened 75 percent of the time, if not more. Talking all the time, or interrogating them, is counterproductive. Kids make sure of that.

It is helpful to tell yourself repeatedly, "Each of our children is unique, is different, is special." It must be appreciated that no two children have ever been raised in the same family. The firstborn has rookie parents who most likely are way too uptight trying to raise a little adult. The next children have more relaxed parents, but they also have to contend with an older sibling who hates them. Commonly, middle kids get lost. It must be appreciated also that no two children are wired the same: their personalities, talents, capabilities, and interests are as unique as their fingerprints. These uniquenesses are to be valued. Every child deeply wants to be cherished as uniquely separate from his or her brothers and sisters.

Sibling rivalry needs to be minimized when one child acts out repeatedly. Simply assume sibling rivalry. The best thing to do is to increase your time with that child, customizing your time to his or her interests. Take just one child along on errands and surprise him or her with a treat. Take just one child along shopping for his or her school clothes. Take just one child to the fast food restaurant of his or her choice. Read aloud to a younger child, just the two of you. Join your teenager to listen to his or her music, asking for the necessary translations, of course. Take one child along on a business trip, tacking on a few days for vacationing.

It is important for parents to celebrate each child's successes. One of the worst things parents can do is tone down their pride in one kid's achievements, fearful of causing yet more sibling rivalry with the others. Recognition of merit, so important in the family's business, has to begin at home. Otherwise, the child feels his or her accomplishments are not valued. This sets up yet more perceived favoritism: "What are you on me for all the time? I'm the one busting my tail at school and in sports. He doesn't do squat, and you let him get away with it. He's coddled for doing nothing, and I end up a nobody around here. It's not fair!" When one child excels, praise him or her. Let no good deed go ignored or undervalued. After one child receives accolades, begin to look for opportunities shortly thereafter to celebrate something of each of the other children. They will be looking for their moments in your sun too.

Sibling rivalry is minimized when parents refrain from bragging about one child's achievements to their other children. It is tempting to tell the child living across the country how well a brother or sister is doing back home in the family business. If it is a fact, and is important to the one outside the business, because of his or her vested financial interest in the company's success, fine, tell him or her how well the sibling is doing. But do so matter-of-factly, and then go on during the phone call to show customized interest in the child on the other end.

Sibling rivalry cannot be minimized if children are forced to work with each other in the family business or are forced to report to a sibling. This is asking too much. The undercurrents will inevitably surface. The most successful family businesses have siblings working in separate areas of the company, with different reporting structures. Some families have split the company up into separate enterprises, with each sibling having bottom line responsibility, risk, and reward. Some have started, or purchased, other companies for their children when they come "on line" in their development to manage. Why force siblings to work elbow-to-elbow because of some unrealistic, sentimental, parental dream of everyone in the family working happily with each other?

One of the fondest hopes parents have is the hope that their children will love each other and will always be close. It is a nice hope, but it is usually not in the cards. Parents love their kids virtually on an unconditional basis. Siblings' love for each other is always conditional. Otherwise, why the common saying, "You can't pick your family, but you can pick your true friends"?

## Only One Coalition Allowed

There is only one coalition inside the family that is helpful. It is mom and dad together as a united front to the children. Mom and dad need to stick together as a team. Why is this a parenting best practice? Because of the three benefits a united parenting team provide to the children.

The first benefit is how the mom and dad coalition provides children emotional security. Kids feel secure when they see their parents being kind and affectionate to each other; when they see their parents discussing things constructively; when they see their parents relaxed and happy to be home. These things tell the children not only how marriage works and how adults can get along together, but also how strong the leadership of the family is. They gain a sense of security from the parental team. These benefits are not possible when parents are divided. They are also, unfortunately, not available to single parent families.

The second benefit of an undivided parenting team is a decrease in chaos caused by every kid's favorite game: "Let's play one parent

off the other." Kids are pros at this, but their success is blunted when
they have to deal with the united front of both parents. Mix-ups and
confusion between the parents, like whether one did or did not grant
or deny permission without the knowledge of the other, are minimized. Telling children, "Dad and I will have to talk this over first,
and then we'll get back to you," and "This is something mom and I
will decide together" sure beats saying to kids, "Go ask your mother,"
or "What did your father say?"

The third benefit of parents being a united team is the most
important. It allows children to be children. This is possible when
the parenting team reinforces the very important generational
boundary within the family itself.[2] On one side of the boundary are
the adults—they are responsible for the family as its leaders, executives, managers. Families are not democracies. Children have a say,
but the parents are management, with final authority. On the other
side of the generation boundary are the children—they are not
responsible for the family. They are responsible for acting their age.
They should not be required to be part of a coalition with either
parent. Coalitions across the generational line are hazardous to the
health of the family.

An example of violating the generational boundary is the
mom/kids coalition versus dad. Dad is never home, so mom seeks
companionship, friendship, empathy, support, and comfort from the
children. They are her sole reason for living. Children in this type of
family become "adults" who are responsible for mom's welfare. They
end up substituting for their absentee father. This division, at the
heart of the family, can harden overtime, leaving the children very
confused and weighted down. Now the children are not simply
responsible for acting their age. They now have to shoulder some, if
not all, of the emotional weight of the family. Their parents have
been unfaithful: dad is married to work, mom is married to the kids.

Adult children stuck in such a family often have a great deal of
difficulty leaving home. If they do leave, they eventually return after
unsuccessfully making a go of it on their own, usually coming home
with a baby or a personal mess for the parents to take care of. It is as

if they are aware of what their failed attempt at independence says: "Maybe this will bring my parents finally together."[3]

Another common coalition that crosses the generational boundary is the coalitions of parent's favorites. These are coalitions of one parent with his favorite kids, and the other parent with her favorite kids. It can be dad with the boys, and mom with the girls. Or dad with the athletic kids, and mom with the artistic. Or dad with the oldest, mom with the rest. Or dad with the kids who are good in school, mom with the slower learners. Or dad with all the children, mom with the baby of the family. Or dad with the robust and healthy children, mom with the child needing special care. And so on.

On the surface, these affinities seem harmless. But too many important and much needed relationships are neglected. These families usually lack the husband/wife team, which is the heart of the family. No family thrives when the marriage is neglected. Then too, each child lacks a complete relationship with the other parent. Parents favoring one or more children add fuel to the fires of sibling rivalry. Children do not feel they measure up to the other parent's favorite kids, deciding they will either never be successful in that parent's eyes, or will have to do something out of character to get closer to that parent. And lastly, this family will not experience family togetherness, the very thing they will wish they had for the family business later on.

These two common coalitions (and there are others to be sure, as unique as all families are) have implications for families owning businesses. There is, of course, the specter of divorce, which is the death of the family. Parents not committed to each other as a loving couple and not united as a parenting team, can easily drift into an emotional divorce. When the kids are finally gone from home, the parents split, resulting in the increasingly popular empty-nest divorce.

Family businesses take a real hit when their owners struggle with the effects of divorce. The energy and concentration needed to lead a demanding business just are not there, the company thus suffering from a lack of leadership. And the havoc caused by the property settlement alone can be an enormous blow to the financial well-being of the family, and its business as well.

Families with coalitions do not have the unity needed as business owners. Owners divided against themselves cannot stand. Owners jealous of each other, favorites versus nonfavorites since childhood, have a devil of a time coming together. Succession of leadership, when the founder is about to retire, is enormously complicated when children have had coalition training since childhood. It is a prescription for chaos and heartache when the founder dies, leaving the future of the business "up to the kids to decide"— children who resent once again having to do what parents failed to do. Where there has foolishly been no estate planning, children who have been in coalitions against each other all their lives are primed for the fight of their lives.

It is best for families to have only one coalition—the coalition of mother and father as a team, whose two priorities in their home life are their marriage and their teamwork as two equally important parents. With parents united, children know they are in good hands, feeling free to grow up unencumbered by the weight of a family on their growing shoulders.

## Help Them Walk Away

If there is one thing that can be said about children, without doubt or fear of contradiction, it is this: children learn to walk to walk away. It is not human nature to remain dependent, to betray our own inclinations, to stifle our own unique voices, or to clip our own wings. By the age of two the battle cries for autonomy are loud and clear: "No!" and "Do it myself!" This begins the quest to be our own persons. Parenting best practices help children walk away from then on.

When parents have done their job well—enjoying their children, telling them important stories, avoiding favoritism, and allowing them to act their age, instead of burdening them with the emotional responsibility of the family—children are able to walk away without rejecting their parents and family. There will be episodes of rejection to be sure, especially by children between eleven and thirty years of age. It is best to regard these episodes as experiments of independence. Children do not really want to reject their parents. Eventually most come around. But they desperately want to be who they are inside and outside— unique persons in their own right. They act as though this is their divine right. They are right: it is.

There are a number of ways parents can nurture their children's inevitable quests for freedom. Parents would do well to enjoy their kids' natural exuberance, rather than quashing youthful passion. It is not good for a child to come to distrust his or her own zest for life, ending up as an uptight, bottled up, uncertain adult. Parents can also encourage their children's freedom by understanding and accepting their kids' feelings, rather than in effect saying, "Don't feel what you feel" or "Don't feel what you feel, feel what I feel" (the old "Put a sweater on, I'm cold" routine), or worse, "Don't feel at all." These stoplights hinder emotional development, and force children to act out feelings, rather than learning to express them. It is better to show children understanding so they in turn can understand the poetry of their own emotions, a necessity of maturity.

Parents can help their children walk away by respecting their children's thinking. Children are almost always very clear thinkers when young—they know the emperor has no clothes, and will tell you so. To ignore children's thoughts or insist they think exactly in confor- mity with parental thinking is to hamper a child from developing a mind of his or her own. Having a mind of one's own is a divine gift, not a synonym for stubbornness. And without a mind of one's own, a person has no chance of ever standing on his or her own two feet.

To nurture children's natural drive to be themselves, parents need to value kids' interests. Who knows why things interest any of us? Surely we all want to pursue what interests us all throughout our lives. It is so much easier to find our niche—where we are really turned on and pumping on all cylinders—when we have internal permission from our parents to pursue our interests.

If children learn to walk to walk away, they would be blessed to have parents who allow them to make their own decisions, even when their decisions are not the ones parents would make. If they make good decisions, the outcome is self-rewarding, and deserving of parents' praise. If they make poor decisions, they have an opportunity to learn from their mistakes, especially with careful parental guidance. The more children practice decision making while still at home with the parental safety net below them, the better they will make decisions when they are on their own. How else can thoughtfulness, problem solving, and decisiveness be learned?

The implications of helping children walk away are self-evident for families owning their own businesses. Those children choosing to walk away from working in the business need to be just as valued by their parents as those children who walk into their family's business on their own. No one should have to be a family business person.

### SUMMARY OF PARENTING BEST PRACTICES

Parenting best practices are designed to help parents meet their children's basic needs. When children's basic needs are met, they do a pretty darn good job with the rest of the adventure of growing up. Five basic needs of children, and corresponding best practices of parenting, include the following:

- The need to be cherished; enjoy your children and have fun with them.
- The need to learn what is important in life, and in their family; tell them important stories.
- The need to be treated as a unique person; minimize the rivalry they feel with their siblings.
- The need to be free to act their age, and not have to carry their family around on their young backs; provide them a united parenting team that takes responsibility for the family's health.
- The need to walk away with permission and encouragement; encourage them to pursue their unique inclinations. Who knows? They may choose to come back and join the family's business someday as contributing adults with their own special strengths and gifts.

## BACK TO THE BASICS

1. Sometime in the next week, approach each of your children separately, and say, "I have two hours sometime in the next couple of days just for you and me. I'll do whatever you'd like us to do. I want to have some fun."
2. Get out your child's baby book, or family photo album, or slides, film, or videotapes, and tell some tribal stories. And admit the hairstyles were indeed outrageous back then!
3. Give each of your children individual attention at bedtime four nights a week for one month; notice any difference?
4. Strategize with your spouse how the two of you can prevent the kids from playing you off the other.
5. On three occasions in the next week, resist the temptation of doing for your children what they need and should be doing for themselves.

## CHAPTER EIGHT

# Honor Your Parents

*People think I am a successful adult. And I feel and act like one, 98 percent of the time. But when I am with either of my parents, or when I am with both of them at their house, or with my father here at the office, I feel like a little kid. I'm sure our employees pick it up, too, even if I call my father by his first name. With my parents I revert back to being a kid again, and they of course revert back to how they were when I was young. They don't treat anyone else the way they treat me. Two Sundays ago, for instance, after we played a round of golf, I was in the clubhouse with my father and the two guys we were golfing with. My father has to always call into the warehouse. He feels important that way. He finds out they're having some troubles, but not enough to call us or anything. But my father yells clear across the clubhouse, "Get the hell down there and clean that mess up. When are you gonna start taking charge for once?" I mean, I just crawled out of there. I was so humiliated. I did hear, though, one of the guys rib my old man about being too cheap to hire Sunday help. God, I resent my old man. I'd just like to . . .*

Anonymous

ALL CULTURES EXPECT CHILDREN TO HONOR THEIR parents. Some, especially Asian cultures, extend this to honoring all elders, whether parents, extended family, or seniors in general. The Judeo-Christian Bible explicitly makes honoring one's parents the fifth of the Ten Commandments, right alongside commandments governing murder, adultery, idolatry, and workaholism.[1] Such is its importance. What people everywhere instinctively feel is that honor is due to those who went through the pain, sacrifice, generosity, and patience required to get a human being to adulthood.

For children still at home, dependent on parents for daily care, protection, and emotional nurturing, honoring one's parents is pretty straightforward. It means respect, obedience, acting one's age, and learning responsibility and accountability. For grown-up children who have left home, however, honoring one's parents is not so straightforward. The imperative has no time limit—it is a lifetime expectation. Even though at times we wish otherwise.

*Your mother is coming again? How long is she staying?*

Anonymous

*Come here and at least say hello. Mom wants to talk with you, and it's on her money. Hurry up! Here he is, mother, he's dying to talk to you.*

Anonymous

*I suppose you're going to clean the garage, basement, and windows now that your parents are coming for the holidays.*

Anonymous

*Now when grandma and grandpa come over for dinner, I want you kids to chew with your mouths closed, and don't say any of those words your daddy's always saying. You hear me?*

Anonymous

*My mom tells me I'm not feeding the baby enough, and yet our pediatrician says the baby cries all night because he's stuffed. I wish she'd butt out, she's not a doctor.*

Anonymous

*I've never been able to please my old man. He's criticized everything I have ever done. Like what I majored in in school. Like the girl I married. How many kids we have, and what we even named them. How we raise them. How we manage our money. I suppose he thinks he's somehow helping when he hands out his report cards constantly. But does he have a clue about why I avoid him? I'd prefer never seeing him again, frankly.*

Anonymous

*I've been in the family business ever since I got out of school. It's been thirty years now. And you know, dad is still the boss, won't listen to my ideas, treats me like I'm a little kid, and distrusts me and my computers in the business as though information technology is a thief. I wish I could just up and leave him and his business. It's not ours. It's his. But I can't abandon him now that he's close to eighty years of age. He's the one who ought to grow up. But he'll never change.*

Anonymous

Clearly, honoring one's parents after leaving home is not straightforward at all.

## WHAT BRINGS NO HONOR

I think it is helpful to consider first what honoring one's parents does not mean to an adult child. First of all, it does not mean staying home. Umbilical cords and apron strings are meant to be cut. Children learn to walk to walk away. Children want to grow up and become grownups. Being a grownup is a better deal than being a child anyway. It brings parents no honor to have children who cannot stand or walk on their own two feet.

It does not mean obeying our parents the rest of our lives. Taking decades to grow up, getting an education, and having outside experiences enable us to think for ourselves, make decisions, and be responsible for our lives. To continue obeying parents is to continue to be dependent on them. It brings parents no honor to have children who do not know what to think or do on their own.

Honoring one's parents does not mean paying our parents back. One of life's harder truths is that parents will always love their children more than their children will ever love them in return. And besides, how could anyone return all the forgotten sacrifices, kindnesses, protection, safety, and favors parents provide their children, especially in the early years? It brings parents no honor to have children carrying around an emotionally charged, heavily indebted balance sheet that can never be paid off.

It does not mean trying to change our parents. Parents are who they are, and it is best not to get too bent out of shape about them. It is equally futile to hold out until they change. What good is there to hold out on a peaceful, appreciative relationship with them because they have not changed? What benefit is there in refusing to make good changes for yourself until they change? It brings parents no honor when children conduct their lives on the wish that their parents change and finally become what the kids have always wanted them to be.

To honor one's parents does not mean rescuing them. Rescuing means doing for people what they have to do for themselves. This is in contrast to helping people: doing for them, and with them, what they cannot do for themselves. Children cannot help their parents' marriage, cannot lift their parents' grief after a loss, cannot prevent their parents' decline with age, cannot design a new life for them, and cannot be responsible for their parents' total happiness. These are things everyone must do for themselves. It brings parents no honor to have their children try to direct their parents' lives.

It does not mean continuing the old battles and grudges. An excellent illustration of this is the dialogue between the daughter, Chelsey, and her mother, Ethel, in the film *On Golden Pond*.[2]

Chelsey: *Why wasn't that old s.o.b ever my friend when I was young?*

Ethel: *You're sounding childish. Of course he was your friend. He's your father. You're such a nice person. Can't you think of something nice to say?*

Chelsey: *He won't be proud of me or my marriage. You know why? Because he doesn't care. He's a selfish s.o.b!*

Ethel: *That s.o.b happens to be my husband.* [slaps Chelsey across the face] *You're wrong about your dad. He does care. He cares deeply. It's just that he's absolutely a muck about telling anyone. I know he'd walk through fire for me and through fire for you too. And if you don't understand that you're not looking closely enough.*

Chelsey: *I don't even know him.*

Ethel: *Norman is eighty years old. He has heart palpitations and trouble remembering things. Just exactly when do you expect this friendship is going to begin?*

Chelsey: *I'm afraid of him.*

Ethel: *Well, he's afraid of you too. You two should get along just fine. Here he comes. Go talk to him.*

It brings parents no honor when children live in their past, as though they were still kids and the parents still in their twenties and thirties.

Most importantly, honoring one's parents does not mean bringing dishonor to the family. This goes without saying, really. It brings parents no honor to have their children conducting their lives as unproductive citizens, losers, jerks, crooks, or people without values and character, who botch up every relationship and opportunity they have. Enough said.

## WHAT BRINGS HONOR TO PARENTS

We honor our parents first of all by turning out right. This can hardly be overstated. By making something of ourselves, creating our own good families, succeeding at the work of our choice, taking good care of ourselves, and being financially self-sufficient, we honor our families of origin.

We honor our parents also by passing along the good we have received from them. Since we cannot ever repay our parents, all we can do is pass it along to our own families, our careers, our community. This is akin to imitation as the sincerest form of flattery. It is not that we are exactly imitating them. It is simply incumbent on us to benefit others the way we benefited from our parents.

We honor our parents by staying in touch with them. It grieves parents to not hear from their children. It hurts them to always have to reach out to their children without hearing from them of their own initiative. Parents feel rejected when children ignore them. They feel guilty anyway for not having been perfect parents. It is worse when they feel shut out. Some parents respond by further isolating themselves from their children, emptying the family of any sense of belonging to each other.

On the other end of the spectrum are parents who intrude constantly, so as not to lose touch. They call daily, if not several times daily, virtually showing their dependency on their kids, as though there is nothing else to live for.

The best way to honor parents in situations like these is for children to do the initiating. Most children will not do this for fear of making things worse. But usually it makes things better. When regularly contacted by their children parents after a while conclude that their children care about them, that there really is not that much more to talk about, and that they do not have to chase after the kids to be simply remembered.

This can be a real problem in family businesses. Some parents near the end of their careers try to make up for their diminishing role in the business by getting into everything. In response, children who are now running things try to isolate the parent, hoping to merely stop the parent's micromanaging. In effect, by trying to keep parents at arm's length children end up sweeping parents into the dustpan of not being wanted, needed, or valued. To honor one's parents by staying in touch with them, in a situation like this, calls for keeping the parent informed, seeking his or her advice, and then setting limits on micromanaging:

*Mom, I would like you to come to the Monday morning executive team meetings. I'd like you to contribute, but please don't dominate the meeting. I'll call you on this if you do, because that's my job. I'll do that with anyone. But we would benefit from your input. Will you come?*

*Dad, I need your advice on this. What do you think? What would you do? What would you worry about on something like this? I will take your input into consideration, but the final decision is mine and our team's. And I expect you to live by our decisions. That's the way it is now. Remember, Dad, you wanted me to follow you, and I'm doing so. Now I am the boss, and you are my honored dad. You get all the glory anyway, you know. That's why everyone still calls you Mister. Some honor, huh? Let me refill your coffee.*

*Dad, put yourself in my shoes. You used to be in them. You wouldn't like it if somebody always is second-guessing you. You never liked Monday morning quarterbacks anyway. I don't want you going around the leadership team and doing things on your own. It creates a helluva lot of confusion among the people. I want your advice and support. You can hammer on me in private, but not in front of others, and not behind my back. I want you to keep your word when I agreed to take the reins—that you'd be a coach and advisor. Not a player. I am asking you to stop doing my job and the job of the other managers. We need your cooperation. I don't want your career ending with people losing respect for you, like some old fighter in the ring one too many times. I love you, but here at work the buck stops with me and my team of leaders. That's the way it is. No exceptions. Let's shake on it again.*

We honor our parents by saying good things about them. It is obviously a good idea to say good things to them directly. But it is even better to say good things behind their backs, especially to people you guess might get back to your parents. There is hardly anything more touching to a parent in family business than to hear from an old friend, "Your kid tells me he's really learning a lot from you, and that he's happy he joined the company." Parents beam when introduced to someone who says in all sincerity, "I'm glad to meet you. I have heard so many good things from your daughter about all the great things you've done at your family's company."

A parent is touched when he or she attends a team meeting at work and hears a son or daughter begin with, "This project is crucial to our company because it fits the dream and purpose my parents had when they started this place forty-four years ago. I'm proud of their dream and our common purpose. It still holds today as it did back then. And we better do it error free, or I'll hear about it. Dad hasn't changed on that either, ha ha." A parent is honored to be in an audience and hear a son or daughter say, "I wouldn't have this opportunity without the sacrifice, leg work, and generosity of my parents. I owe them a debt of gratitude. But since I can't repay them, I'll make sure we'll do everything we can to go forward successfully."

We honor our parents by bringing out the best in them. If they are happiest working, we can have projects galore ready for them when they visit our homes. Accomplishing something together promotes closeness. If they are talkers, not listeners, we can encourage them to talk, especially about what they know best, their past. So what if we have heard all the stories before? Effective listening can help us connect things that are good to know. If they are more free of bad habits outside their home, then we can invite them more often to our homes. Parents usually conduct themselves better when they are our guests. On their turf they are the parents, and we are the kids again—an atmosphere conducive to old habits.

If they like to help, then we can ask them for help, especially in areas where they have expertise.

An excellent example of bringing out the best in one's parents is occurring in a family business where the founder started out as a mechanic. After building a $70 million company and retiring, he was asked by his successor son if he would like to help out in the machine shop. The son feared that retirement for a man with no hobbies could be deadly. And he did not want his father to spend his days trying to still run the company. Besides, there was a real need in the machine shop, especially with the development of new machinery. The father has been in the machine shop for several years now, absolutely enjoying himself. The only ownership prerogative he insists on is eating with the executive team at their regular noon meetings—he claims the food is better than in the company cafeteria (he's the only one at the table wearing coveralls).

The point here is that it is O.K. to turn the tables as a way to honor our parents. They wanted what was best for us when we were little. Now we can bring out their best and provide moments in the sun for them. In their honor.

There are two important ways to honor our parents that have already been discussed. One is to forgive our parents for being young when they had so much influence on us, for being products of their own backgrounds and times, for having good intentions without knowing how to deliver, for struggling with pressures on them that children are not privy to, and for in fact being rookies everyday when it comes to being parents. The other way is to keep things peaceful and enjoyable. This involves seeking enjoyable things to do together, refraining from refighting the past as though the past can be changed, and creating a reservoir of new good memories that can give you courage to finish some unfinished business between you and your parents.

There is one more way to honor our parents. It involves finishing unfinished business before it is too late. Usually this means finally saying "I love you" before our parents die. In some families saying "I love you" is like trying to swallow an elephant whole. In some families it will be the most courageous thing ever said. But everyone wishes they had said "I love you" sooner than later, at least once.

Sometimes unfinished business means saying to parents "Thank you." Not just for raising us, but for giving us pride in what the family has accomplished—the family business. Gratitude to parents involves appreciation for giving us a head start with our careers, funding our educations, giving us permission to pursue our own interests, or giving us the opportunity to work within the family's business to take it to its next level.

Unfortunately for some families, finishing unfinished business means discussing some old hurts that still cause pain. Forgiving one's parents would be greatly assisted if a child could ask his or her parents what was meant by something said, what was going on at the time something happened or did not happen, or what the parent would have done differently if they could do things over. These discussions could enable the child to see the parents as more under-standable, more vulnerable, and more human than the child's hurt could allow previously.

A good example of this is the family whose middle child grew up feeling like an orphan in the family. His role in the family business was always a forced one—a square peg in a round hole. When he at long last sat down with his parents to discuss his feelings as an outsider, he learned why his parents did not provide him the necessary, nurturing attention he so needed and craved during his most formative years. They finally told him why. They revealed the unspoken tragedy of their family. When he was four, his nine-year-old sister was killed in a car accident while on vacation with some family friends. The driver, who was the father of the vacationing family, was intoxicated. His sister was the only fatality. Neither parent had been able to forgive themselves for allowing their daughter to go on that vacation, especially since they knew the man liked to drink. Since the parents could not comfort or support each other in their excruciating grief, they each had had extra marital affairs that blew up in their faces. All this was happening when their son was between four and nine years old. They admitted to having emotionally ignored him, because their own wells were dry and dirty. The parents told him they had always loved him, and had always wished they could do things over. Upon learning all this, the son saw his parents in a different light. A new more positive and close relationship began between them. The son eventually left the family business, free at last to pursue his own interests, because he finally felt he was valued by his parents. He showed his parents honor by finally reaching out to them. And they reached back. Unfinished business completed before it was too late.

## SUMMARY

The cultural and religious imperative to honor our parents is a crucial family matter. For grown children, honoring our parents, "that our days may be long in the land which the Lord our God gives us," as the Fifth Commandment promises, means . . .

- Becoming the best possible persons we know how to be

- Passing along to our family, business, and community the good we have received

- Staying in touch with our parents

- Saying good things about our parents, to them as well as to others

- Bringing out the best in our parents while there is still time

- Forgiving them for having been young and all too human when they had the most impact on us

- Keeping things peaceful and enjoyable, in order to build good memories

- Finishing unfinished business with our parents, before it is too late

## BACK TO THE BASICS

1. Send a birthday card to each of your parents, even if it is not their birthdays, telling them five things you have most appreciated about them.
2. Ask your parents for advice or help on something for which they have expertise.
3. Invite your parents to discuss what was easy and what was difficult for them while you were young, listening to learn and to show understanding.
4. Just once, let something slide that your parent says that normally you would try to correct, debate, or defend—it is better to be close than to be right.
5. Muster up the courage to hug your parents and say "I love you."

## CHAPTER NINE

# Permission to Succeed

*The thing is, I did better in school than anyone else in my family, even in classes where girls don't excel, like math and science. And I'm the oldest child. But I'm the only daughter. So I got cast into the "take care of everyone" mold, including taking care of my baby brothers. They were prized by our father, in sports especially. To this day I'm shy about beating anyone, whether it is badminton in the backyard, or playing bridge. It's like I don't want to hurt anyone's feelings. So you guessed it. My brothers are in the family's business. Very successful, nice guys. I love them. And I ended up a nurse, taking care of everyone, including doctors, who probably had worse grades than I ever had. It's like no one ever told me I could be whatever I wanted to be. Or that it's O.K. to win at anything. I'm thinking of a career change, given all the changes in health care. Trouble is, I don't know what I want to be when I grow up, ha, ha.*

Jeanie, RN, age fifty-four,
daughter of founder,
electrical contracting company

I HAVE LISTENED FOR COUNTLESS HOURS OVER THE YEARS
to business and professional people talk about their struggles with being

successful. I have worked closely with families having one or more family members in their business who are less than the success anticipated. From these experiences I have come away with the following observation: fear of success is more common than fear of failure.

Success feared? On the face of it, it does not make sense. It is counterintuitive. You would think everyone wants to be a winner. After all, the success industry—motivational speakers, books, tapes, videos, conferences—is a nine-figure industry annually. But the success industry proves the point. People struggle with success.

The struggle with being successful is surprising, given how parents groom their children to succeed. Parents spend fortunes on their kids' education, sports, wardrobes, health, and crooked teeth. And every family business seemingly was created by founders who wanted the next generation, and succeeding ones, to have a head start on success. Unfortunately, being successful is no easy thing for far too many people. For some, it is the central psychological issue of their lives.

## A FEAR-OF-SUCCESS STORY

The oldest son of a family-owned auto dealership had been running the business for four years. He was the third generation president. His father had successfully expanded his father's start-up by adding several lines of high-quality imports, and had always pushed for an honest, efficient service department. Father also instituted a board of directors two years prior to his semiretirement. He wanted his son to have guidance and accountability. The board was comprised of a banker, an accountant, an attorney, two prominent local businessmen, and a successful car dealer from another state, one of father's old college friends.

The son was college educated, majoring in business. He had worked for his father since high school, from washing cars out on the lot to eventually becoming a salesman. Early in his presidency, the dealership won an award from one of its major automakers. The award for excellence was predicated on the years of his father's efforts. The son, however, took all the honors, accepting the award himself at the convention, excluding his father from the publicity photos. Since that award, the son pursued other awards and publicity with a vengeance, using key office personnel to spend inordinate amounts of time filling out awards applications.

The son took no interest in the nuts and bolts of the business. He was bored with finances and the service department. He loved the front of the business. He was the consummate glad-hander with customers, employees, fellow country-club golfers, and community leaders. Increasingly he got involved outside the business, from becoming president of his country club to becoming president of his service club. He said yes to everything outside the dealership, and increasingly no to everything inside.

He procrastinated on the need for computer updates and new shop equipment. He had audits done by a very close friend. He was always late for meetings, but made an issue of any employee's tardiness. And he got involved with a secretary—first helping her financially because she was poor, then taking her to lunch at his club after the lunch crowd was on the golf course, and finally taking her on numerous business trips to dealers' meetings. Since he was recently divorced, he felt blameless.

No more awards were forthcoming. The service department became riddled with customer complaints. Sales started to slip. Employee turnover exceeded industry and local standards. Nevertheless, he pushed the board for huge increases in compensation because of his divorce settlement and high-flying lifestyle.

The board was a soft touch at first. For sentimental reasons. The son's pay raise was granted, disguised as an adjustment. And the board approved his request for expensive consultants. In response, the son became a walking dictionary of management fads. He could not speak without mentioning paradigms, empowerment, teams, process analysis, gap analysis, Pareto diagrams, just-in-time inventory, total quality, and reengineering. After two years of this wheel spinning, the employees were deeply cynical—there was no leadership for implementation of the consultants' work, and no follow-up and follow-through on anything started.

In spite of all the management-speak, the son did not change. He was still late to everything, still procrastinating, still glad-handing, and still ignoring needs for organizational infrastructure. When he split the sheets with the secretary ("we didn't have enough in common"), he and the company were served a sexual harassment petition by the scorned woman. The board's hand was finally forced. Reluctantly it exercised its leadership responsibility by removing the son from the company—with a saddened father's consent. With a substantial golden parachute, a "reward" for being a family member, not for being a winner, the son moved out of town and became a fund-raiser. The board saved the company, for the sake of the rest of the family and for the employees. Sadly, it could not save the son from his compulsion to fail. He set it up to be dishonorably discharged. The son was afraid of success. His behavior proved it. He sabotaged himself.

The son had been promoted to a job for which he was not prepared. His sales experience was no apprenticeship for executive leadership. He was in way over his head and did little to correct this. He was self-serving, going for glory and attention as a substitute for substance. He wasted time, energy, and money—his own—and, worse, others'—on non-essentials. His priorities were on peripherals. He lacked gratitude and humility, standing on others' shoulders, especially his father's, without giving credit or benefiting from their counsel.

As executive leader, the son got on the slippery downhill slope by committing the two cardinal sins of business: he ignored the customer, and he failed to build an organization responsive to customer needs. Simply put, business is, after all, making promises by sales personnel, and delivering on the promises by the rest of the organization. The young man overpromised, and underdelivered. The dealership could not deliver with a service department in turmoil, an inadequate finance department, and an outdated, inefficient information system. Then too, the son ignored classic storm warnings: turnover, slipping sales, and customer complaints. The son would not say no to outsiders, but failed to say yes to correcting his own organizational needs.

As do so many persons in leadership positions, the son worked a couple levels below his current position. This was especially true when he was under pressure. He reverted back to what he was good at—charm and sales, only thinly disguising his underdeveloped leadership skills.

The board of directors had to share responsibility for this. Directors wrongly treated him as an entrepreneur—someone who does business on gut instincts and sheer force of energy and personality. This dealership was well beyond the entrepreneurial stage. It needed professional, executive leadership. The board was remiss in not collaborating with the son, and his key personnel, on goals, requirements, expectations, standards, and accountability, all measurable and binding, with a mutually agreeable timeline. Consequently, the son took advantage of the lax board, gaining more time and money for his own agenda.

The son's agenda had not included self-improvement or leadership development. As a substitute for leadership, he practically in desperation looked for magic. He, of course, found none in the management fads, in the consultants, or with his secretary/girlfriend.

Regarding the stupidity of dating a woman inside the company, let alone someone over whom he had organizational power, the son at this point was clearly asking to get canned. This was his loudest plea of "Kick me!": setting the board up to do what he would not do himself—getting him out of a situation in which he was sabotaging himself because he was afraid to succeed.

## SELF-SABOTAGING BEHAVIORS

People who fear success indulge in all sorts of self-sabotaging behaviors. They do themselves in with all sorts of behavior that simply rub others the wrong way. They lose other's respect, trust, confidence, and patience. After indulging them once too often, others finally give self-sabotaging people what they have been asking for, a swift kick of rejection.

Self-sabotaging behaviors of the fired auto dealership president included:

accepting a position for which he was not equipped, and doing
  nothing effective to develop the needed skills;
not knowing or doing the critical top priorities of his job;
lacking respect for those who contributed to his opportunity;
not seeking, inviting, or accepting others' input;
ignoring storm signals;
pretending problems will go away, or can be put off;
finding substitutes for substance;
seeking magic;
serving self only;
wasting his and others' time, energy, and money;
ignoring or abusing his customers;
overpromising and underdelivering;
refusing to admit one of life's basic truths: work means solving
  problems;
almost always having trouble saying no;
avoiding accountability;
using people for his own gain;
being chronically late, with disruptive consequences;
procrastinating, especially putting off what is important;
not growing, learning, expanding, changing—he still was what he
  was;
violating the law;
turning people who care against him by "asking for it."

There are other common self-sabotaging behaviors besides the ones exhibited by the fired son. It is not uncommon to see people afraid of success who:

screw up just prior to a promotion;
screw up once they have gotten to the top;
do important stuff poorly;

refuse to listen;

refuse to talk straight;

refuse to be open with their thoughts, needs, wants, and feelings;

vent their anger, frustrations, and negativity whenever and wherever they feel like it;

deny there are problems;

admit there are problems, but claim they are either insignificant or
so huge that nothing can be done about them;

admit there are problems, but claim they do not have the people
or the resources to do anything about them;

do not stay informed about their industry, marketplace, or
competitors;

do not keep their word;

do not meet timelines;

refuse to be organized;

cannot find important documents and paperwork because their
office and desk resemble a teenager's bedroom;

refuse to be computer literate;

abuse alcohol, drugs, or money;

succumb to a victim or entitlement mentality;

do not return calls or respond to mail and memos;

do not show appreciation;

do not speak up when things do not seem right;

pursue petty things, especially office politics and gossip;

play the blaming game, instead of problem solving;

charge off with knee-jerk reactions time and again;

flit around from one number one priority to another—"priorities
du jour";

raise people's expectations and hopes, only to let them down;

do not follow up or follow through;

play not to lose, rather than play to win;

let their opponent or competitor pass them by;

do not let themselves win very often, if at all;

feel sorry for the next guy, always;

take on everyone else's responsibilities, jobs, or problems;

get themselves chronically overwhelmed by volume of work;

are overly ambitious, especially at other's expense;
take all the credit and never the blame;
take all the blame and never the credit;
are lazy at work;
run out of gas when their car's fuel tank reads empty.

## FEAR OF SUCCESS

Losing behaviors are symptoms of a fear of success. Why do people fear success? There is no one explanation. It is a topic that has fascinated the fields of psychology, sports, and business for a long time. Freud even wrote about "those wrecked by success."

Why people fear success is as personal and unique as their fingerprints. But nonetheless, because there are so many people struggling with being successful, some generalizations can be made about cultural, religious, social, and psychological influences.

### Cultural Influences

There are cultural influences against being successful. Our culture gives all kinds of mixed messages about success. On the one hand, it trumpets success, but on the other, it trashes successful people. Successful people are made sport of—their accomplishments are diminished by criticisms, scrutiny of things personal, celebration of flaws, demeaning jokes, and the assumption that anyone successful is so because he or she is crooked, or ruthless, or undeservedly lucky. Our celebrity worship prevents the emergence of true heroes. And we continue the ancient practice of not honoring a prophet in his or her own hometown—anyone getting off the plane with a briefcase is considered more of an expert and a success than some local yokel.

Then too, our culture has a bias for the underdog, for blue-collar effort, for the common man, and for the egalitarian approach, that somehow has been equated with the average. To stand out successfully is to invite derision. Successful people are called "big shots," "big wheels" (and "you know what dogs do to wheels," as the old saying goes), "mucks," "suits," or "someone in the big house" (alluding to slave owners). And successful people should be punished with heavy taxation, according to class warfare campaigns in politics.

All this cultural prejudice is experienced early in life. Woe to the child in school who does his homework, knows the answers, gets A's, and excels in extracurricular activities. Teachers too often protect the lesser achievers by not allowing the stars to shine in class. The brainy ones are considered geeks and nerds. Special attention and special education, with all its resources, usually only go to the disadvantaged, and kids with losing behavior get enormous attention, from counseling to tutoring. Winners fend for themselves too often.

In spite of our underdog bias, however, our culture has traditionally discouraged true underdogs from succeeding, whether by tolerating poor inner-city schools, or by erecting glass ceilings in the workplace—there are not very many "Smith and Daughters" even in the world of family businesses.

Our culture also does a disservice to the definition of success. It narrowly equates success with position and money. This equation is a far cry from persons using their interests, talents, and skills doing something they love without sabotaging themselves. Anyone pursuing work that does not yield status or wealth is assumed to be underachieving at best, or unsuccessful at worse. The homemaker and especially those who work with children—from teachers to pediatricians to babysitters—are paid poorly and accorded little esteem. The thinkers, the artists, the tinkerers, the barbers, the gardeners, the low-profile craftsperson, the small- time shopkeeper are not the subject of success stories. Neither are those who are content to do their jobs well day in and day out with no designs to get into things beyond them. And yet so many of these people are successes in their own right—they at a minimum do not derail themselves with self-sabotaging behavior.

Finally our culture, especially the business community, simply does not know what to make of people who limit their careers because they want to balance their personal and work lives. Almost weekly the business press publishes articles on executives, women especially, who step down to be better parents. Men who job share with their wives, so they can be true fathers, are newsworthy oddities. Employees who quit jobs requiring extensive travel because they want to have a home life are dismissed as not ambitious enough to "do what it takes to get ahead." Our traditional operating definition of success remains—if you want to get ahead, sacrifice everything, including your family.

## Religious Influences

In addition to cultural influences, there are religious influences that take a rather jaundiced view of success. An impressionable child nurtured on the following biblical warnings could clearly have a devil of a time dreaming one day of being important and successful: the mighty shall be brought low; think yourself to a sober judgment of yourself; money is the root of all evil (kids rarely hear that it is the love of money that is the problem); the young rich ruler did not choose the Kingdom of God; the wealthy farmer died as a fool after setting up his retirement; the poor widow is lauded in contrast to people of power who are seen as selfish; and it is easier for a camel to go through the eye of a needle than it is for a rich man to enter the Kingdom of God.[1] The darkness of all this obscures all the other "let your light shine" messages of religion, leaving far too many faithful in an uneasy cloud of guilt about being successful, or wanting to be.

## Social Influences

The social inhibition to being successful is colorfully summarized by the last century journalist, Ambrose Bierce, when he said, "Success is the one unpardonable sin against one's fellows." It must be a social sin to be a success. Otherwise why the prejudice? It goes like this:

> *Now that he got promoted, he thinks wonders what he is. He's too good now to hang around us commoners. You watch, he'll move to*

*the better end of town, he'll start driving a foreign car, he'll chase*
*all over for gourmet food, and announce how he and his family are*
*going to Europe. I mean, people go to Europe just to brag that*
*they've been there. Like in their stupid Christmas letters. Who the*
*hell does he think he is? I knew him when, and I know darn well*
*he still puts his pants on one leg at a time. Mark my word, he'll buy*
*things he doesn't need, with money he doesn't have, in order to*
*impress people he doesn't like. Nothing worse than the newly rich!*
                                                    clichés of the jealous

What this litany of clichés represents even permeates family
life. The sibling who succeeds more than the rest of the family
members is commonly the object of jealousy, sometimes even from
parents who are still struggling with their own lack of success.
There is no one lonelier at a holiday family gathering than someone
who is more successful than everyone else in a family of nonwinners or losers.

### Psychological Influences
This brings us to the most powerful influence on whether
someone will embrace or fear success—the psychological influence
parents (and teachers) have on children. The formative years are
long, lasting through early high school at least. Children almost
always make life-determining decisions during this period that
enable them to survive. These life-determining decisions are made
deep within, below the child's awareness. From there the decisions
exert virtually lifetime influence unless changed.

It is rare for a child to risk going against the grain of parental
influence. Survival is at stake. So children take the safe route, even
if it means going along with parental role modeling and messages
that add up to "don't succeed and don't be important." Kids who
receive this message do not see their parents role modeling a work
ethic. They hear their parents trash their jobs, their employers, and
the "system." They listen to their parents complain how unfair and
stacked against them everything is. They seldom see parents solve
problems by thinking rationally and constructively. They seldom see

parents read books, newspapers, or watch anything edifying on television. They hear their parents lament, "If only we had . . ."

Children decide to fear success also when they are the targets of the following abusive judgments:

"You'll never amount to anything!"

"What's the matter with you anyway?"

"You screwed up again. Once a screw-up, always a screw-up!"

"You take after that side of the family. They've never been worth a damn."

"Why can't you be like your sister and other kids? They pay attention. You're just a damned knucklehead."

"Don't be talking big ideas around here. Our people don't get into that sort of stuff. Remember who you belong to."

"You're just a dreamer. Come back down to earth, boy. You'll never make it anyway. We never do. Best is to settle for something steady and safe."

"So you wanna be a big shot, eh? What's the matter? Aren't we good enough for you anymore? You too good to put your feet under our table? Huh?"

"You're getting big headed. Too big for your britches. You'll be cut down to size soon enough. Then you'll fit back in around here."

Some children are not given these red-hot branding irons. They are derailed from achievement by living in a disheveled home with disheveled people who aspire to nothing. Or they are coddled with, "That's O.K., honey, if you don't feel like doing it. If you don't feel good, then just turn on the TV in your room. You can do your homework tomorrow. You can stay home." Or, "What do teachers know anyway? Don't sweat it. You can't learn much from books anyway."

Role modeling and messages such as these from parents (and/or from teachers), combined with cultural, religious, and social influences, are almost too much for most children to rebel against in order to be successful. They make decisions, usually below their level of awareness, to adapt to all these stop signs. They want to be accepted instead.

They want to survive among people crucial to them, whether they be family or peers with similar baggage. They spend the rest of their lives living down to their parents' and peers' expectations, living up to their parents' and peers' predictions, and proving their parents and peers were right all along. This is fear of success.

## FEAR OF SUCCESS IS MANY FEARS

Most people with a fear of success are not aware of their fear. They do not wake up in the morning and deliberately set out to sabotage their potential for success. They do not necessarily listen to a small voice in their heads saying, "Don't succeed and don't be important." They do not admit that success is not for them. Rather, they struggle with more conscious fears that betray their fear of success. The most common fears people consciously struggle with include:

- Fear of betraying loved ones; this is the most powerful fear—they fear they will be rejected and abandoned if they become more successful than their loved ones
- Fear of never being able to measure up to a parent, especially the parent who is most successful by society's standards
- Fear of incurring others' jealousy
- Fear of being different, even though their interests and talents in fact differ from those of family and friends
- Fear of responsibility that comes with responsible positions
- Fear of risk taking, lest predictions about failing come true
- Fear of finally making it—"then what?"
- Fear of the spotlight, which does not blink at vulnerabilities
- Fear of peer rejection and criticism—successful people are fair game
- Fear of loneliness; it is lonely at the top
- Fear of no longer belonging to their old group
- Fear of growing up, realizing that the carefree freedoms of adolescence and young adulthood can be no more

- Fear of hurting others, either by passing them up, or beating them as opponents, thereby crushing their dreams
- Fear of power, especially power over people's lives
- Fear of hard work and the sacrifices required for becoming and staying successful
- Fear of money, with its bad reputation and responsibility

Conscious fears like these, that provoke self-sabotaging behaviors, are the wolves at the door of those who fear success.

## THE REST OF THE STORY

Why did the car dealership president sabotage himself after finally making it to the top? Why did he sabotage his golden opportunity by taking the dealership his grandfather started, and his father built up so excellently, to the edge of ruin? Why did he fear success? Because he was not given permission to succeed, especially by his parents. Even though he had such a golden opportunity, the son was no different than anyone else. In order to succeed, he needed permission.

His father was essentially an absentee father, devoting himself night and day to building the dealership. He had high work standards that he not only imposed on himself, but also on everyone else, including his family. At home he was thus dominant and controlling. His wife, naturally, was quite the opposite—sweet, gentle, passive. She doted on her son and younger daughter. She protected the children from her husband's harshness. Both kids ran to her when their father was tough on them. Her softness essentially contradicted the father's standards. In reaction, father oversteered and overcorrected to prevent the kids from being spoiled.

The son, being the oldest and hence the most parented, received a continual double message that amounted to "don't succeed." He could never live up to his father's standards, and he did not have to measure up to any standards from his mother. He acted out to get his father's attention, getting dealt with harshly (negative attention is better than no attention), only to be coddled by his mother immediately thereafter. This would precipitate a fight between his parents, a fight for which the son would feel guilty. The repetition of all this over time reinforced the son's decision deep inside—"I screw up everything."

Blessed with good looks and a quick mind, the son developed a strategy of charm to make it in the outside world. In school he was the class clown. His grades were middling, because were he to be an academic star he would not have been as popular. He was a lonely kid at home and needed friends badly. Teachers slotted him grade after grade in the "charming, not very serious" category. They figured they could not challenge him successfully; when they did he rebelled by underachieving (just as he has been responding to his father's challenges). His teachers, therefore, in order to achieve maximum classroom peace and quiet, never pushed him again. It figured that college was a four-year fraternity beer bust. After all, he had a job waiting for him, and he already was driving a new imported car—his father was occasionally generous with things.

Why did the father take him into the dealership? Family tradition, and guilt. Family tradition—third-generation male with the family name on the big sign out in front of the dealership for another thirty years. Guilt—maybe now after twenty-two years of neglecting him, father could finally get close to his son—fathers do mellow over time. In his heart of hearts, however, father knew this would be a long shot. The kid had been an underachiever forever, but maybe now he would grow up and start achieving, especially because the two of them would be working together.

Sadly, success was not in the cards for the son. He almost consciously believed he could not do the job his father had done. He lacked confidence that he could meet father's demanding standards. If he did surpass his father, he almost consciously would have feared betraying his mother (by being like his father), and would provoke his father's and sister's jealousy. So he feared success, sabotaging himself, and taking his life script to another town. The one thing he needed he did not get—permission to succeed, especially permission to succeed from his father.

## Permission from Father—How?

How could father have given his son permission to succeed? There are several ways. First, father needed to create a relationship with his son like never before. Simply telling or preaching "you can do it" does not get very far. Permission to succeed does little when a relationship is broken. Without the beginnings of a meaningful relationship with his father, the son could not get over his anger for his father (his exclusion of his father at the awards ceremony was an angry example), or forgive his father for being so harsh and setting such high performance standards.

To begin a meaningful relationship, father could join his son golfing, where the son could finally beat his "old man," as he called him behind his back. The father could refrain entirely from criticism or making suggestions on the golf course. At the nineteenth hole, and in subsequent get-togethers, father could begin to show his human side. He could relate how frequently he himself made mistakes or struggled with the business. He could talk of the difficulties he had working with and succeeding grandfather. He could point out where he trusts his son, what he values about his son's people skills, and what the son had been doing well. Again, father would have to bite his tongue—no criticisms or suggestions. Father in effect would be moving closer to his son, creating an adult-to-adult relationship. He would slowly build up to becoming his son's partner at work.

To become his son's partner, and eventually his mentor, father could remove himself from the board of directors during portions of its meetings when it dealt with executive leadership issues. The board members could then, in a businesslike fashion set measurable goals for the dealership and the son. Father then would be making himself available to his son as an "outsider" to the board's directives, offering to serve his son as a partner and mentor regarding board requirements. By doing so, father would be on the son's side for the first time.

After all this careful relationship building, father and mother could sit down with their son and finally finish up all their unfinished business before it is too late. It would be crucial for the parents to present a unified front to the son, especially by being affectionate to each other. This would take the son off the hook of feeling he has to take care of his mother. The message father especially would need to convey could go something like this:

> *I wish I would've known how to be a better father. If I had it to do over again, you and I would've done more together. And I would've told you at least once that I loved you. But before the inevitable happens, as we refer to kicking the bucket in our family, I'll say it now. I love you. And it's O.K. with me if you sell the business, or keep it, and take it further than I could. I'm behind you all the way.*

The message mother would need to convey could go something like this:

> *I want you to know that your father and I have a big, long trip planned for next month. We're reading everything we can get our hands on about the places we'll see. Your dad read the funniest story to me last night. We're already having fun. When we get back we're going to start looking for property to build a retirement place. We're both eager to begin our new chapter together. We're both very excited.*

This breakthrough would give the son what he never experienced before: affirmation from his father, permission to succeed, and parents who are together as friends. The son is finally free to be an adult, rather than a child rebelling against his "old man" and taking care of his mother.

## GETTING PERMISSION TO SUCCEED

There are truly blessed people who get permission to succeed at home from an early age. Their parents do such things as:

- Take genuine interest in their children's interests
- Listen carefully to their children's thoughts, feelings, imaginations, and dreams
- Applaud their achievements
- Read to their children, and listen to them read
- Take a keen and active interest in their school experience
- Expose their children to life's incredible variety
- Give age-appropriate responsibility and decision making
- Set high but reasonable and age-appropriate standards and expectations
- Correct mistakes without hurting feelings
- Give plenty of latitude for trying things
- Show understanding and forgiveness for mistakes
- Stick to appropriate consequences for irresponsibility
- Role model optimism about the future
- Speak well of work and its possibilities and rewards

When parents give permission to succeed in ways such as these, within the context of a close relationship, children grow up not only knowing that they can make it, but they know that it is in fact O.K. for them to make it.

People who do not receive this generous type of parenting when they are young can genuinely benefit from a breakthrough experience with their parents later on in life. Families can emulate the breakthrough conversation illustrated above with the auto dealership family. Not many parents, unfortunately, are courageous and humble enough to do such good parenting work. This is usually so because they do not know how to go about doing it. Many probably need permission themselves to go ahead and begin building a new relationship with their child, giving him or her the long-needed permission to succeed. Here is where effective family business consulting can lend a hand (see Selecting Outside Help, pages 215–17, for guidelines on selecting a family business consultant).

If parents refuse to go through what it takes to finally give their children permission to succeed, or if it is too late because the parent died before finishing old business, or if the child did not receive permission elsewhere, then counseling would be in order.

Fortunately, there are other sources of permission to succeed besides parents. Some people receive permission for the first time at school. Many successful people credit a particular teacher or coach who essentially gave them permission to succeed. A good employer, especially a good supervisor or manager, can teach people how to succeed, especially by providing responsibility, goals, training, accountability, praise, recognition, and rewards. A good marriage and the responsibility of parenthood can for some persons amount to permission to succeed, stimulating an underachiever, for example, to grow up and work against his or her internal grain for a new life.

Good friends who are winners in their own right can be permission givers. They see the potential in their friend, and are unwavering in their encouragement and steady support. Their own successful examples can be a powerful influence. Persons seeking permission to succeed can also select an admired, successful person as a mentor, or an informal group of admired, successful persons as a board of advisors. Their enthusiasm, challenges, and goal setting can make a profound difference for someone performing a level or more beneath interest and talent. Self-help literature can also jump-start a quest to be more successful, although the inherent limitations of going it alone with books and tapes usually need to be overcome with the help of constructive, augmenting relationships.

No matter the sources of permission to succeed, everyone still has to repeatedly throughout life echo that permission to himself or herself: "It's O.K. for me to succeed. And I am going to! I'm willing to do what it takes, because what it takes will have its own rewards."

## IMPLICATIONS FOR FAMILY BUSINESS

We have established that the family serves the business, and the business serves the family. Both. Successful family businesses are committed to both propositions. This means the family makes every effort to raise children who are unafraid of succeeding, and who, if their interests, talents and skills fit the family's business, then the business will be in good family hands for another generation. And if the business serves the family by providing the wherewithal to educate its children, and provides work opportunities right up the children's alleys, then the whole family will earn the bounty of their successful labors. Everyone wins in a family where no one is afraid to succeed, regardless of the vicissitudes of the business world.

## SUMMARY

Everyone needs permission to succeed. There are so many obstacles to success, from cultural, religious, and social confusion about success, to the lack of guarantees that education will set children up for success. Further obstacles include parental influences that unwittingly derail children, and early work experiences that show little vested interest in employees' success. Somewhere along the line people need permission, a green light among all the red lights, to fearlessly pursue their interests, talents, skills, and energy, pursuing what they love without sabotaging themselves.

## BACK TO THE BASICS

1. List five ways each of your parents demonstrated success in what they did and how they approached life.
2. In what ways have your family members kept themselves from achieving their potential?
3. Go ahead and win at something—it is O.K. to beat someone in a game.
4. What are your real interests and real talents? What jobs or careers fit your real interests and talents?
5. List five undesirable consequences if you succeed at what you would really like to do; list five desirable outcomes.
6. Repeatedly say to yourself, "It's O.K. for me to succeed. And I'm going to!"

# ─CHAPTER TEN─

# Resolving Grief

*Thank goodness all of dad's affairs were in place and easy to take care of. And the help received from our business attorney, accountant and insurance agent proved invaluable. The minister was O.K. in the beginning, but like everyone else, he disappeared after the first few weeks. Actually, we all thought we were doing fine, until about just before the holidays. It was three months after dad died. It seemed like we all got worse. At our family's business, mom got involved like never before. She got all businesslike. Unapproachable. My sister and I were uncharacteristically irritable with each other. At home, mom withdrew, and refused to talk about her and dad. And my sister and I tried to protect our own families from anything too emotional. We tried to get through the holidays with stiff upper lips. It took my three-year-old daughter to remind us of our humanity. At mom's house on Christmas day she asked several times, "Grandpa coming?"*

David, age thirty-seven, vice president,
cement and gravel company

IT MAY SEEM UNUSUAL TO FIND A DISCUSSION ABOUT grief in a book about family business. But the focus of this book is family matters in family business. And grief is a family matter, a powerful one, that affects not only all family members, but also the family's business. I have worked with family business owners whose founder had died, whose wife and mother of the founding family had died, whose family had been torn apart by divorce, and whose founder had mentally died due to dementia, particularly Alzheimer's disease. These families were thrust into bewildering ups and downs of grief without a grasp of what was normal and helpful. Their quiet, highly personalized sadness led them to struggles, behaviors, and decisions that unnecessarily complicated their inevitable roller coaster experiences.

## OUR INEXPERIENCE WITH GRIEF

There is widespread lack of appreciation of what grief entails. It would be reasonable to assume that an understanding of grief is universally common knowledge. After all, no family since Adam and Eve has ever been exempted from the hard work it takes to successfully grow beyond the loss of loved ones. And yet, particularly in America, most of us are relatively inexperienced with death. Thanks to modern medicine and the absence of war on American soil, many of us live many years before a death occurs in our immediate families. This is an experience gap that earlier generations did not have, and people of other countries do not have. We are more familiar with the death of a marriage and family, given our miserable divorce rate. We seldom associate grief with divorce, although families go through a difficult grieving period well after the papers are signed. The same can be said of the increasing number of families suffering with a member befallen by Alzheimer's disease—their grief is slow and long, yet seldom appreciated.

Thus, when any kind of death occurs in a family, essentially inexperienced people must come to grips with their losses, struggling in quiet, solitary ways. Most lack the support previous generations received from extended families, close neighbors, religious ritual and tradition, and visitations of friends beyond the first month after a loss. Grief turns out to be a stranger to most of us, even though it visits us all eventually.

I will outline the broad range of feelings and behaviors that are common after significant losses. I believe that family members deserve and need a basic understanding of what grief is normally like. After losing a loved one, we would benefit from having a reassuring, informed voice in our heads telling us that we are not cracking up, but going through what is normal with grief. We need to know what to expect, so we will not be scared or worried about the feelings and behaviors of a grieving family member. We will less likely abandon the bereaved if we know something about their grief experience. To mismanage grief is to live as though the living are dead, and the dead are living.

## Grief Is Natural

Grief is natural. As the old saying goes, "Only people who avoid love can avoid grief." Grief after death, divorce, and dementia is not a weakness, a psychological disorder, a mental illness, a spiritual stumble, or a minor blip on the screen of life. No matter how hard-hearted or chickenhearted we are, grief hurts like hell. And it is inescapable. There are no substitutes for it, just as there are no substitutes for any kind of suffering. No amount of pretending that there is no hurt at all, no amount of stiff upper lips, no amount of keeping it all bottled up, no latching on to someone else immediately as a substitute, no hundred-hour work weeks, and no amount of drinking or taking medications can replace the grief experience. When it comes to grief, the first of the four noble truths of Buddhism has particular resonance: "Life is suffering." Grief simply has to be lived through and worked through as constructively as possible. By all family members.

## THE WORK OF GRIEF

Grief is hard work. Calling it work means some things have to be accomplished, lest grief goes unresolved. Unresolved, grief leads to the living acting as though they were dead, and treating the departed as though they are still present. Four things need to be achieved.[1]

## Acceptance

The first task of grief work is to accept the full reality of the loss. It is normal in the beginning of grief to pretend that the departed will return or that there will be a reunion sometime in the future. With divorce, there is the fantasy of recreating the marriage and family in ways that repeatedly proved impossible before the family's demise. With dementia, there is the wishful thinking that the loved one is just getting a little older, no more than that. And for some there is also the tendency to discount the importance of the loss: "Oh well, that's life. Tough. I won't let it get to me."

Eventually, however, the finality of the loss and its meaning become hard realities. Yes, life goes on, but the loss is permanent. And final. Acceptance of this cold reality is made tougher for the divorced, since the main players still have to relate to each other, especially around children, grandchildren, and money. And it is made tougher for families whose member has Alzheimer's disease because the afflicted can live for years in an ever-deteriorating state. All grieving persons have to work hard to reinvest their lives in a new chapter of life without the lost person.

## Experiencing Pain

The second task of grief work is to experience the pain of grief. This is a bitter pill to swallow. Losing a loved one is painful, period. Trouble is, we all are conditioned to avoid pain. The last thing we want to do is admit to ourselves, let alone to others, how much we are hurting. So we push away and push down our painful feelings, mistakenly thinking that if we do not admit our loss, the pain will go away. It will not. It is best to allow ourselves to cry out loud, openly curse our fate, talk about the things that are missed about the lost loved one, and feebly put into words what the lost person meant to us. We need to remember that feelings and thoughts eventually have to come out anyway, preferably through words and tears, and not through physical illness or self-defeating behavior. All grieving persons must reduce their pain over time by experiencing it, so they can begin their new life chapter with energy available for living, rather than energy wasted in the futile attempt to keep the pain of grief buried deep down.

## Adjusting

The third task of grief work is to adjust to the environment in which the lost person is missing. This means living without the lost loved one. Whatever the lost person did will no longer be done, unless the grieving person picks up the slack, fills the vacancies and the emptied role. For some this means taking over the family finances for the first time. For some it means taking care of oneself, from meals, to laundry, to auto care. For some it means parenting solo. For those in family business, it means succession to executive leadership, or regaining customer confidence, or making major strategic and capital decisions for the first time, or facilitating owner-ship meetings for the rest of the family.

Adjusting to the new environment also means making tangible changes in the home, and/or at the office. I worked with a widow who kept her deceased husband's medications on the kitchen table for three years; a widow who kept her husband's garage the way he left it the day he died four years earlier; a widower who kept his wife's expensive clothes in her closet for three years, including perfume and jewelry on her vanity as though she would be returning soon; a family business that kept the founder's office as though it were a museum, never to be used again by anyone, except his ghost of influence. These sad persons fostered the myth of the deceased as still living, rather than doing the hard work of learning how to effec-tively fill their environment without the lost person.

## Reinvesting Emotions

The fourth task of grief work is withdrawing emotional energy for the lost loved one and reinvesting it in other relationships. Persons who do not accomplish this claim they will never love again, either out of loyalty to their departed intimate, or out of self-protection, not wanting to be hurt so deeply again. Some divorced persons allow themselves the indulgence of bitterness, nursing grudges at the expense of new, more positive relationships. Others try to short-circuit their grief by rebounding into another relationship before their mate's body is cold, as the universal expression puts it, or before the ink on the divorce papers is dry. This rebounding seldom works in the long run. The new intimate is swindled, not only by having a relationship with a grieving person who cannot possibly be himself or herself so soon, but also by being used as a ghost of the lost love.

Some persons fail to reinvest in other relationships because of the conflicts it can cause with their children. Teenagers and adult children especially resist their parents' new friendships, whether platonic or romantic. Some even try to micromanage their parent's lives by complicating matters to such an extent that a new friend is driven away.

Completing this portion of grief work means the grieved person begins to love again, without diminishing in the least their gratitude for all the good they enjoyed with the departed loved one. To love again means investing in closer relationships within the family, in old and new friends, and perhaps eventually in a new intimate. To love again does not mean having loved the lost person any less.

## WHEN IS GRIEF FINISHED?

When is grief finished? Not for a long time, usually. Too often people assume grief is a short-time thing, a month or two at most. Grieving people receive an outpouring of sympathy, cards and letters, flowers and gifts, visits and generous amounts of food for a couple weeks or so, and then are essentially abandoned. They are seen functioning pretty well at work and are assumed to be over the worst of it. Their one or two days of bereavement leave from work is assumed to be sufficient.

This could be true for those who lose an elderly grandparent after a long illness. But it could not be more unrealistic for those who lose a spouse, a parent early in life, a sibling, or even a close friend. And it is unrealistic in the extreme for those who lose a child, or lose someone due to unexpected tragedy, especially suicide, the cruelest of all losses. Grief in these circumstances is at a minimum a year-long process. Most studies show that fewer than half of all widows are themselves again at the end of the first year.[2] It is not much different for widowers. And three to four years of grief over the loss of a child is to be expected.

I consulted a family business where one of its key employees lost his only daughter to a tragic incident at college. In true male tradition, he returned to work the week after her burial and performed heroically for a couple of months. But his work performance began to unravel as the Christmas holidays approached and her birthday passed. Management had been generous with its sympathy, but became impatient with him during the dead of winter—always the toughest season. By spring they were ready to let him go, exasperated that he was not his old self. Fortunately, the family owners were willing to learn how grief is a long-term experience, and how vital it was that grief counseling be encouraged, since the grieving father had not opened up to anyone. I feared, had they fired him, that his family would have had another burial to attend. And the family business owners would have mourned their mistake.

So when is grief finished? Hopefully it can be finished within a year or two, after the grieved person has gone through the seasons and meaningful events of the year. But in order to be finished, the grieved person has to have done the hard work of completing the four tasks of grief work discussed above, enabling the bereaved to

> think of the deceased without pain (and to think of the divorced ex-spouse without bitterness). There is always a sense of sadness when you think of someone that you have loved and lost, but it is a different kind of sadness—it lacks the wrenching quality it previously had. One can think of the deceased without physical manifestations, such as intense crying or feeling a tightness in the chest. Also, mourning is finished when a person can reinvest his or her emotions back into life and in the living.[3]

## THE NORMAL GRIEVING PROCESS

Grief is such a highly personalized experience that no two persons mourn exactly the same way, even in the same family. And a Wisconsin German farmer will grieve differently from a New York City Italian, an urban Jew differently from a rural Swede, a teenager differently from her grandmother, a hard-boiled person differently from someone outwardly more sensitive. Grief too is different after an infant succumbs to sudden crib death than after the death of a four year old, different after a prolonged illness than after a car accident or a suicide. But the differences of grief are not so dramatic that we cannot benefit from generalizing about very human responses to loss.

Normal grief reactions include many different emotions, physical reactions, thought patterns, and behaviors that ordinarily were not experienced prior to the loss of someone loved.[4]

### Emotions of Grief

Grieving persons commonly ride an emotional roller coaster. Up one minute, down another; up one day, down another; up all work week, down on the weekend; up for a few months, down during emotionally charged periods surrounding special calendar dates. The emotions of these ups and downs include:

***Numbness/shock***: lack of feelings right after the loss; it is a natural mental protection from becoming overwhelmed

***Relief***: a positive feeling of comfort after an ordeal of long suffering

***Sadness:*** an incredibly painful emotion from deep within that cannot be put into words; only tears and crying can express the unexpressible; not to be suppressed—crying is beneficial both emotionally and physically

*Anger*: almost always present, although confusing; anger for being left behind, for past hardships, for past wrongs, for being left with a mess of things to do solo; sometimes misdirected towards doctors, hospitals, God, children, the other woman or man, or towards self

*Guilt*: commonly for feeling that everything that could or should have been done to prevent the loss was not done; for not making things right while there was still time, like saying "I love you," or apologizing; for past mistakes and failures never resolved

*Loneliness:* a battle with being alone in an empty house and empty bed; a sense of isolation from the rest of the world; a yearning for the missed person; a yearning for everything to be wonderful again, even though it may never have been so; having to go to usual places and special events as a single person

*Fear:* from a light sense of anxiety to strong panic attacks; fear that we cannot make it alone without the lost person, fear we cannot take care of ourselves, fear we cannot manage things without the lost loved one, fear of our own mortality—that our own days are surely numbered too

## Physical Reactions of Grief

Since we humans are made of "spiritual tissue," it is little wonder that grief's emotions are felt physically. So much so that it is not unusual for grieving persons to suffer some sort of illness, from colds, to flu, to more serious health problems. Elderly widowers have a higher death rate the first half year after losing their wives than men their age who are not widowed. Short of illness, people in mourning commonly report appetite disturbance, sleep difficulties (difficulty falling asleep, early morning awakening, and vivid dreams of the departed), weakness, shortness of breath leading to frequent sighing, tightness in the chest and throat, and a hollow sensation in the stomach.

## Thought Patterns of Grief

There is little question that grief throws people's thinking off. Ordinarily clear-headed persons can become less rational, less common sensible, more impulsive. They have difficulty organizing their thoughts and trouble remembering where they put things. This absent-mindedness and befuddlement are new experiences. The mental energy drain of being preoccupied with the lost loved one is new also. Some grieved people pour over pictures, personal effects, events, sayings, and experiences of the lost relationship, even to the point sometimes of eerily experiencing the presence of the lost person. Fortunately in normal situations, the sensation of seeing, hearing, and feeling the lost person subsides within a month or so.

It stands to reason, then, that grieving persons are less capable of making solid decisions during their mourning period. This is why there has long been the advice to grieving persons: "Don't make any major, life changing decisions immediately. Don't move, don't change jobs, don't remarry, don't even get entangled in a rebound relationship, don't sell off the business. You have enough on your hands coming to grips with your loss and your new circumstances. Let well enough alone for now. The time will come for major decisions. Trust yourself then."

## Behaviors of Grief

In addition to not eating and sleeping well, grieving persons commonly withdraw socially, preferring the safety and comfort of home. They get sick and tired of answering well meaning questions of friends and acquaintances about how they are doing. They would just as soon spare others the awkwardness of their own discomfort around grief. They do not want to be a social drag on friends, or upset the social balance of couples by being the lone single tagging along. And they do not want to cry in public. If this social withdrawal continues past several months or so, grieving people can slip into a deeper apathy. This requires hard work to reverse, lest months of bleakness become habitual and so comfortable that little energy is available for reinvesting in life again. It is better for grieving people to do what is good for them, whether they feel like it or not.

### The Roller Coaster Experience

To visualize what grieving people normally go through, it is helpful to picture the typical first year as a roller coaster. The roller coaster begins its descent as the loved one's health declines, or the marriage begins to unravel. At death or final separation/divorce, the grieved person plateaus, thanks to numbness and relief perhaps, and support from family and friends. Usually by the third or fourth month, however, there is a deep plunge—numbness is replaced by the full realization that the departed is gone forever. Social support usually has now disappeared because "he/she is doing just fine, adjusting so well." This third to the fifth or sixth month period is the most painful and difficult, the bereaved being most vulnerable to making poor decisions, rebounding into a premature relationship, or slipping to self-neglect.

If the grieving person continues to work on the four tasks of grief, the roller coaster takes an upturn, until there is a major, meaningful calendar event. Then it is down again, although not as low as the third

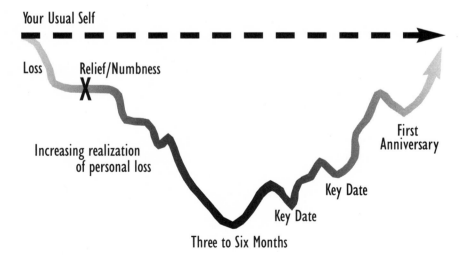

or fourth month trough. Minor ups and downs continue, although the adjustment work pays off with an upward trend. As the first year ends, the grieving person gets closer to being himself or herself again, although the anniversary of the loss may be a temporary downer. There is social custom and some religious practices, particularly in the Jewish faith, that sanctions one year as the "official" end of the mourning period. As was pointed out above, however, there are many situations of grief that go into a second and third year. The roller coaster is tamer, however, with more high points and shallower troughs.

What grieving people normally go through is thus not simple at all. It is a painful conglomeration of emotions, physical reactions, thoughts, and behaviors that are new for them. All this is natural. Again, it is not a weakness, mental illness, or spiritual failing. It is just plain grief. It is understandable and deserving of being understood.

## A Note about Depression

It is important to understand that grief is not depression. Whereas grief is natural and to be expected, depression is a psychological disorder, whether a self-defeating reaction to bad circumstances, or a brain chemical deficiency, or a combination of both. Although people use the word "depressed" glibly to describe their garden-variety blues, it is best to reserve the word for the painful condition depression is.

It is true that the typical symptoms of depression are similar to grief: sleep and appetite disturbance, low energy and fatigue, poor concentration and diminished work performance, loss of interest in things that normally give pleasure, loss of sexual interest and energy, social withdrawal, and an overall sense of guilt, for actual or imagined deeds and for feeling so useless. Grief, however, lacks two hallmark depressive symptoms: an overwhelming sense of worthlessness, and self-destructive behavior. Self-destructive behavior can be severe self-neglect, substance abuse, reckless pursuits, suicidal gestures, and even suicidal behavior. Truly depressed people who are suicidal are pathologically angry and take the anger out on themselves: "I'll get you even if it kills me," "I'll do myself in and you'll be sorry," "You've killed me, so I'll finish myself off." It has been said that every suicide is a misdirected homicide.

Most grieving persons can work through their months or years of mourning with the help of friends and family, work and play, religious faith, and true grit. Depressed persons do not readily benefit from these kinds of help. Their condition warrants professional assistance: mild conditions from talking therapy, moderate and severe conditions from a combination of beneficial medications and talking therapy.

## A Note about Divorce

The death of a family is no less a tragic loss than the death of a loved one. Divorced spouses and family members mourn their losses in much the same ways as grieving a death. But in many ways, their grief struggle is made more arduous. Society is much more casual, if not even cavalier, about people's loss of their family. There is no outward religious support; sometimes there is condemnation instead. There is little if any outpouring of sympathy, gifts, phone calls, help, food, or empathy. Visitations and invitations to dinner are seldom practiced.

Extended families are only reluctantly pressed into duty for performing roles now abandoned. They do not fly across the country to be with their grieving family member, as they would in the event of a funeral. And there is little appreciation of and support for the daily heroism of the working single, divorced custodial parent.

This casualness toward divorced persons is not all they have to endure. They still have to somehow maintain a relationship with their departed former loved one—whether financial, or what is much more difficult, having to continue as parenting partners. Children and grandchildren, no matter their ages, make divorce so much more diffi-cult. And it must be remembered that children are in grief as well.

All this is not the worst part of having to still relate to the plaintiff or the respondent, as former loved ones are called in divorce papers. The whole adversarial nature of so-called family law is emblematic of what differentiates divorce from death in peoples' grief reaction—it is betrayal. Divorced people feel betrayed, because betrayal is at the bottom of their loss. Their lifetime vows—"'til death do us part"—have been betrayed, as have countless other promises and dreams. Fidelity has been betrayed, whether it is the infidelity of self-centeredness, or to career or another person. The partnership is betrayed. Their shared coping skills, problem-solving skills, and mutual accommodations, worked on so hard over the years, are finally betrayed. And all pleasures and joys once shared will no longer give wings to the heart—betrayed. Whereas the death of a loved one is a loss, the death of a marriage, and consequently the death of a family, is a failure borne of betrayal. This makes divorce grief work so difficult.

## WHAT GRIEVING PERSONS CAN DO

There are several general things people going through the ordeal of grief can do that can prove helpful. Among them are the following:

Listen to that small voice in your intelligence that tells you what you are going through is natural and normal for anyone belonging to the human race.

Talk out your feelings—to yourself, your Maker, your friends, your family members—anyone who can and will carefully and effectively listen to you.

Let people be good to you, even if they are somewhat awkward, uncomfortable, or unsophisticated about grief.

Swallow your pride and ask for help, for yourself and for your children; save your pride for when your new life chapter is well along.

Take good care of yourself like never before, from eating regularly to exercising daily, from resting to returning to things once enjoyed—all whether you feel like it or not.

Expose yourself to things of beauty, assurance, and inspiration, in the faith that life is worth living.

Do not use any of your children as a crutch, a surrogate spouse, a parent, a spokesperson, a go-between, or a scapegoat; let adult children be good to you, but remember that grieving younger children need parental nurturing and limits from you and others, not parental dependence; the elderly are the exception, needing to appropriately depend on their adult children.

Remind yourself that the dead are not living, and that you are not dead.

## WHAT OTHERS CAN DO FOR THE GRIEVING

Family members and friends are usually in a quandary about what to do for grieving loved ones. We do not know what to say, what should and should not be brought up, what amount of leaving them alone is best, how often we should contact them, or to what we should invite them.

We cannot go wrong when we do the following:

Hug them.

Listen carefully and caringly to them, so their story unfolds, so they feel understood, and so they learn some things about themselves and about your caring.

Never interrupt them or change subjects when they begin talking about their situation or feelings.

Never try to smooth things over when they are talking by offering such palaver as, "There, there, everything will be all right," "Time heals, so don't dwell on the negative," "Cheer up, better days are coming," or "Pray about it and everything will be fine."

Do not abandon them: call them frequently, visit them regularly, invite them over for meals, drag them along to places and events you know they enjoy or would enjoy.

Offer them concrete, practical help; from the mundane of everyday living, to the complications of finance, insurance, and law; but especially, offer help with the children—grieving parents and children deserve breaks from each other.

Reassure them that they can count on you, that what they are going through is to be expected, and that you believe in them.

## A NOTE ABOUT ALZHEIMER'S DISEASE

As the population continues to age, we will increasingly be faced with families struggling with the loss of a loved one to conditions resulting in dementia, the most common of which is Alzheimer's disease. As of 1996, already four million persons were afflicted by it. Ten percent of persons over sixty-five, and almost half of all persons over eighty-five, have the disease.[5] This will be uncharted waters for many families, except that their grief will be all too human, just as those grieving death and divorce.

The prospect of Alzheimer's disease as a family business issue is increasingly likely, especially in those families where the founder or senior executive later in life does not hand over the reins to the next generation of leadership. The following is increasingly experienced.

Key managers of a family business secretly met to discuss their concern for the seventy-four year old founder/owner/president of their company. Out of sensitivity and some fear, they did not invite the founder's two children, who worked in the company. Several major contracts had recently been lost due to the founder having lost key documents that had awaited his signature. Over the last year he had been steadily centralizing his power and control over practically everything in the company. Key personnel had been fired or stripped of their responsibility by him as he increasingly came to distrust almost everyone. All key indicators of the business pointed to a downward slide.

These key managers began to trade their observations. The founder had forgotten decisions he had made. He had been questioning things employees were carrying out, forgetting he had earlier instructed them to do so. His office and appearance had become more and more disheveled. He had difficulty using cue cards made for him at recent presentations. His driving was becoming erratic and dangerous. He became uncharacteristically rude and temperamental with everyone, including his closest friends. And his vocabulary had become increasingly vulgar, especially around women, causing the managers to fear sexual harassment charges that could stand up in court. In the end, they concluded the company would be ruined over the next year or so if their founder were to continue deteriorating. Did he have Alzheimer's disease, they wondered? The managers, of course, could not make a diagnosis of Alzheimer's disease. Only physicians, especially neurologists, aided by neuropyschological testing, can make a diagnosis of Alzheimer's disease, currently doing so accurately 80 to 90 percent of the time. But the managers observed that the founder's behavior closely resembled the ten warning signs of Alzheimer's disease:

1. Recent memory loss that affects job skills
2. Difficulty performing familiar tasks
3. Problems with language
4. Disorientation of time and place
5. Poor or decreased judgment
6. Problems with abstract thinking
7. Misplacing things
8. Changes in mood and behavior
9. Changes in personality
10. Loss of initiative

What could the managers do? Doing nothing would be immoral, as well as a poor business decision. Aggressively confronting the founder would be damaging to him. It would be an overload he could not handle, except by being aggressive in response, only to sink into more of his own private grief. In the early stages, the elderly have awareness of their diminished capacities—they grieve their loss in much the same ways as discussed above.

It would be advisable for the managers to first meet with the founder's children, who undoubtedly are aware of their father's condition and are more than likely confused as to what to do. They probably are afraid of their father anyway, especially this past year. They themselves need to be carefully and caringly listened to—they are in the early stages of grief themselves over the mental death of their father. Once they feel understood and are convinced of the decent motives of the managers, they need to hear straight talk about the peril their father and the company face. They need to hear the projected bleak consequences of denial and inaction, lest their father's dreams for them and for their family's business come to naught. And then a course of action must be agreed on.

A course of action could be a family meeting with father, when he is told an appointment has been made with his primary care physician because "we are worried, and love you, and want to make sure everything is all right." If it is decided that a family meeting would be too much for father to handle, someone whom father trusts needs to be enlisted to get him to the doctor. Or a ruse, such as an "executive health screening" that the company has signed up for, could be used. The physician should be called or visited beforehand by the children, so adequate time for a thorough examination can be scheduled, and so that the doctor is heads-up about the family's fears.

From this point on the father, the family, and the family business employees are at the mercy and skills of the professionals. Alzheimer's disease cannot be handled by any family on its own. Professional medical help is an absolute necessity.

It is important to remember that this family, including the father, will go through a long period of grief, just as those who grieve the loss of a loved one through death or divorce. They deserve the same consideration and help.

## SUMMARY

Families in business together are not exempt from the hardships of loss, whether by a death of a family member, a divorce in the family, or a brain disease that afflicts an elderly member. They are thrown into a period of grief, usually lasting a year or longer, on top of their continuing responsibility of having to run the family business during this difficult time.

Because so much is at stake—their livelihoods, the livelihoods of their employees, the needs of their customers, the economy of their community, and their hopes for future generations of owners, family business owners need to work through their grief as constructively as possible.

Working constructively through grief is immeasurably aided by an appreciation of what grief entails. The more a family knows what to expect, what is normal, what is dangerous, and what is helpful, the more likely they will be to emerge on the other side of grief, proving to themselves, their employees, their customers, and their community that there is indeed life after death.

## BACK TO THE BASICS

If you have suffered a loss:

1. Find someone you completely trust and tell him or her what you are experiencing.
2. Accept invitations to dinner; it is good to get out of the house.
3. At the end of the one-year mark of your loss, write out why you miss your former loved one, why you have hard feelings for him or her, why you appreciated that person, and how you are going ahead to fully live without him or her. Keep this "letter" to yourself in safekeeping.

If people important and dear to you are grieving:

1. Invite them over for dinner.
2. Listen to them.
3. Contact them on their important calendar events.
4. Insist on lending them an appropriate hand when and where they genuinely need help.

## PART THREE
# The Family's Business Tools

## CHAPTER ELEVEN

# The Family's Values

*I'm glad my son and daughter took over the business when they did. I'm happy to be on the sidelines. One of the biggest reasons is how much more difficult it is to manage and supervise a lot of today's workforce. They just don't seem to have the same work ethic as people did when we got started. You've got to practically spell out what an honest eight-hour day of work is. They like to show up late, spend the first twenty minutes or so in the coffee room, leave for long fancy lunches, and spend company time on personal phone calls. My generation wouldn't have thought of doing all that. And they spend so much time yakking about bonuses, incentives, and all the legal stuff about their rights. Don't get me wrong. The majority are good. But they even want to get out of here one minute before 5:00 P.M., and when we need to get a big project done, they don't want to come in on weekends at all. I don't know, should we have to tell people how to behave? It used to be enough to just tell people what to do.*

Willard, age seventy-one, founder,
pump and irrigation equipment company

IT IS READILY APPARENT THAT THE PARENTS OF
today emphasize different values than parents did three generations ago. In an unheralded, but revealing study called
"Middletown"[1] (it was actually Muncie, Indiana), 141 mothers in
1924 were asked which traits they most emphasized in rearing their
children. The top three endorsed traits were loyalty to church,
strict obedience, and good manners.

Sixty years later the same number of mothers in Muncie, still
very much Middle America, was asked the same question. Today's
mothers valued the traits of independence, tolerance, and thinking
for one's self. Studies in Germany, Italy, England and Japan suggest
similar trends. In three generations there has been a dramatic shift
in what parents value—from high value placed on conformity to high
value placed on individualism. This shift in parental values is evident
throughout our society. This is not our father's world.

Since parental values are so profoundly influential, it is imperative that families owning their own businesses take a good, hard look
at what they truly value. Values are like tools. They shape, build,
drive, and determine the success of both the family and its business.
It is not a question of whether a family business is values driven.
Every family business is. What is valued determines the quality and
outcome of any relationship and endeavor. The question is what
values are practiced, and more importantly, what values are the most
effective tools to build a lastingly successful enterprise.

Two very different family businesses illustrate the profound
influence of values.

## ABANDONED BY CUSTOMERS AND EMPLOYEES

A father and two sons own and operate a family business with
sixty-four employees and $7.5 million in annual revenues. Revenues
are down from a high of $10.1 million three years earlier. Father is
heavily involved in community affairs and trade association activities.
The sons claim that, despite all this extracurricular activity, father

still runs the show, having to make all the decisions, both big and small. One son is the national sales manager, going on the road monthly. He sports a four handicap in golf, has an excellent gift of gab, and can sell anything on the golf course. The other son is the controller, having an associate degree in accounting. He protects the family money down to the penny, bristling over his father's purchases and large political contributions. He argues monthly with his brother over expense receipts not turned in, and over the amounts his brother spends entertaining on the road.

Because of the alarming three-year decline in sales, the father decided to have, for the first time ever, an internal "health of the company" inventory conducted. Interviews with family members, all employees, and a random sampling of customers turned up critical problems.

Interviews with customers revealed little satisfaction. They pointed to sales, especially those by the son, that oversold what the company could deliver. They did not perceive the product as adding much value to their businesses. They were frustrated by the company's phone system. They were put on hold too long, then finally routed to voice mail. When they did get the chance to talk to a real person, the customer service representatives would usually say, "I'll have to get back to you after I check with them. It's not my decision." Or worse, "I'm sorry, but that's our policy." Or worse yet, "I'm sorry for taking so long to get back to you, but there isn't really anything we can do about it."

Interviews with employees helped to explain the 25 percent annual turnover rate. They pointed to the absence of orientation and training, the verbally tense atmosphere, the below-market wages, the absence of a pension plan, the family "union," and dad's ostentatious purchases flaunted in front of the company, including his $86,000 car parked by the front door.

Interviews with both sons pointed to leadership difficulties. They held a dim view of their employees. They decried employees' bad attitudes, the pettiness of their gripes, and the constant demand for wage increases. They were frustrated with their father's lack of trust in them, since he was still making all the decisions. And they agreed with the employees that the atmosphere, generated by their father's intimidating style, inhibited open discussion.

In his interview, father spoke of how he would like to retire, but "The boys aren't ready yet to take the bull by the horns. They better step up to the plate and start working better together." He stated how much he enjoys community work after so many years of doing the same thing all the time. He lamented how customers and employees just were not loyal anymore. And he allowed that "meetings and training are all well and good, but damn, we don't have the time or money to be sitting around at meetings talking about business, when we should be out doing business!"

What values drive this family business? The interviews show ten things valued, nine things not valued.

### Valued:
1. The business is for the family and not the other way around
2. Family togetherness
3. Social skills: they are friendly, nice, fun people
4. Gut instinct: it has brought them this far
5. Courage: entrepreneurs and sales people are gutsy
6. Control via hierarchy
7. Image and symbols of success
8. Enjoyment of the good life
9. The short term
10. Community and political service

### Not Valued:
1. Problem solving: three years of declining revenue, high turnover, brother's expense account
2. Family closeness: impossible when one brother is set up to control the other brother, especially regarding money
3. Knowledge and education: neither for themselves nor for their employees
4. Honest, open communication: neither between themselves nor with customers or employees

5. Employees as partners
6. Trust: everything is forbidden, unless expressly permitted by dad
7. Loyalty: neither to nor from customers and employees
8. Merit: pay is low regardless of performance; rewards for father and traveling son continue regardless of downward trend
9. Responsibility with authority: father has all the authority, but little responsibility for day-to-day performance; everyone else has responsibility, but no authority to make decisions that would enhance performance

It is not constructive to throw stones at this family. They are delightful, good people. But the fact is this family is being judged very harshly by its customers and employees, the very two constituencies without whom their family business cannot survive, let alone succeed. What this family values will not serve them well as they try to reverse customer loss and employee defection. Their values do not bring out the best in their own relationships, in their customers, and in their employees. This family business stands in sharp contrast to an extremely successful entrepreneurial company in Jacksonville, Florida, Physicians Sales and Services, that has as its core the requirement of "never losing a good customer or good employee again."[2]

## EMBRACED BY CUSTOMERS AND EMPLOYEES

A second generation team of brother and sister run a $44 million a year, eighty-three year-round employee company having two independent divisions—food processing and food exporting. Collectively, growth on an annual basis has been averaging 15 percent the past four years.

The founding couple is now retired. They had run their enterprise as a single company, exporting everything they could produce. But they did not want their children to have to work side by side, or have one be either responsible for or dependent upon the other. The two divisions were thus created, with each child having separate authority and bottom-line accountability.

The son, after having finished his engineering degree and deciding on his own to join the family business, was made head of the food processing division. He reported to his father who was chairman of the board, a board that included his mother and three outside directors.

Five years later the daughter joined the family business. It was her own independent decision to return home. She had finished law school and had lived abroad for two years. She was fluent in Spanish and Portuguese. Because of her international experience, fluency in three languages, and legal knowledge of contracts and business law, she was made head of the export business. She was under no obligation to market her brother's products. It was clear to both children that their business relationship was to be strictly business, although both parents secretly hoped their children would favor each other's business.

Both the processing plant's employees and the traders have average salaries for the area, but enjoy a matching 401K pension program, full-range health insurance coverage, and an incentive bonus plan. Both parents still come around with the quarterly bonus checks, something they very much enjoy doing. Employees at exporting receive extensive, one-on-one training from the daughter, who admits she neglects her own work during prime office hours "because if I am the only one here who can work with growers, processors, buyers, agents and shippers, I'll end up doing it all and we'll go under, or I'll go nuts, whichever comes first." Work in the processing plant, while highly seasonal, is run by a veteran crew that is able to attract seasonal help that returns summer after summer.

At a companywide meeting prior to the busy season, employees voiced their desire for a performance feedback system. They wanted to know how to improve, and felt that going the extra mile went unrewarded by the current incentive plan. The need was also felt by the daughter, who was frustrated with one trader who had on several occasions been rude to customers and to coworkers. The management teams of both divisions wanted a better performance feedback system as well. They were cautiously willing to go along with the idea that they would get feedback on their leadership performance from the employees. Their response was a quote from the founding father, "Everything's got to be fair and square."

What does this family value? Twelve values drive this company.

***Valued***:

1. The business is valued as a business and a responsibility, not as a family privilege: the use of a board of directors, the son's and daughter's preparation for employment, and the employees' benefits
2. Family closeness: minimizing sibling rivalry, still involving parents
3. Accountability: board of directors, performance feedback
4. Merit: son and daughter qualified for their positions, incentive bonus plan, endorsed performance feedback system
5. Education and training: for family members and employees
6. Trust: son's and daughter's autonomy; employees trusted once they are trained
7. Respect: for customers' cultures and languages, for customers' needs, for employees' needs
8. Open communication: companywide meeting, employees spoke up, management team invited feedback on its own performance
9. Loyalty: veteran workforce at processing plant
10. Problem solving: employees' complaints and trader's rudeness responded to
11. Fairness: "Everything's got to be fair and square"
12. Profit: bottom line responsibility of each division, incentive bonus program, and the 401K plan

This family is driven by what it values. The father would claim that he does not know any better. He and his wife simply never believed there was a difference between personal values and business values. Their values, coming from deeply held beliefs had to transfer

to their family's business. There was no other way for them. They
believed in family, in business, in people, in customers' right to fairly
get what they pay for, and in employees' right to be treated fairly.
They believed in success and in all honorable ways to achieve it.

What they discovered over the years, and what their son and
daughter are continuing to discover, is that business driven by values
is good business. They did not practice their values at work to be
virtuous. Or to seek attention. Or to be politically correct. Or to gain
advertising advantage. They just felt it was right. And besides, values
in the workplace work. It is a simple truth. People, whether family
members, customers, or employees, want to do business with people
driven by what brings out the best between people. In other words,
constructive values.

## VALUES, IN OTHER WORDS . . .

Values are not easy to talk about. They stretch language as they do
behavior. Consequently, here are many ways to try to say the same thing.

*Values are:*
tools to bring out the best in people;
ways to treat yourself and others that promote mutually beneficial
     relations;
the highest common denominators of behavior, rather than bad
     habit or the laws of the streets and alleys;
ways to conduct yourself that will earn you trust and respect prac-
     tically anywhere in the world.

*Values are:*
the green, yellow, and red lights of behavior: with green you get
     somewhere that you and fellow travelers feel good about; with
     yellow you think twice, learn, discuss, and then proceed with
     caution; with red you stop dead in your tracks, because you
     know you eventually will crash and burn;

the best standards of performance;

the guidelines about what is constructive and what is not constructive to personal life, family life, and work life;

the framework for decision making.

### *Values are:*

best practices at home and work that are time tested and proved;

principles that replace the norms of conduct with the best of
personal and business ethics;

the compass that has been guiding people over the ages to success
over the long haul and to peace of mind;

the hard drivers of all that is good.

### *Values are:*

what people can use to govern themselves without needing to be
treated as little kids;

the performance link between the ideals of aspirations, intentions,
and mission statements and the realities of getting there;

the behavior expectations to be hard-nosed about—not for a
minute are values soft, gushy, or touchy-feely;

what parents want their children to live by, and what they themselves want to be remembered as having lived.

## HOW TO FIGURE OUT WHAT YOU VALUE

I strongly recommend that each family and its employees sit
down together and put into writing what they believe brings out the
best in people. Admittedly, every family and every business has
implicit values that shape their character and behavior. But to get
everyone on the same page and have everyone lifted to the highest
common denominators of behavior, it is beneficial to make what is
desired explicit. In black and white. For guidance. As a reminder.
For encouragement. As a measurement. For growth and improvement. As a higher order conscience.

Families and family business employees can identify what they value and what they would like to have valued by discussing the following sets of questions:

1. List three examples where the worst was brought out in people. What was going on? How were people treated? How were people acting? What brings out the worst in people?
2. Repeat the above exercise for what brings out the best in people.
3. List three times when you were especially frustrated, disappointed, or angered. What was going on, and not going on?
4. List three times when you were especially pleased, exhilarated, and proud. What was going on and not going on?
5. Imagine you have been asked to re-create on Mars the very best attributes of family life and business life. What would they be?[3]
6. What traits do you most emphasize in raising your children? (This is the question of the "Middletown Study.") In other words, what kind of adults do you want your children to become?
7. If you could start a new family and a new company from scratch, what would be the green lights, red lights and yellow lights of behavior for each? Green is encouraged, applauded, demanded. Yellow is discussed and mutually decided, with risks accepted. Red is not O.K., period. Don't go there.

Good, open dialogue about these and other questions of your own will reveal themes of what is held firmly, looked up to, and valued. It is best to boil the themes down to one word each, followed by a brief explanation or example. Five values is usually optimal—enough to be inclusive of most family members' and employees' input, but not too many to memorize.

The purpose, after all, of putting your values down in writing is to have all family members and employees have the tools of lasting success. They deserve a clear understanding of what is expected of them and others, in order to bring out their best and to bring out the best in others.

## WHAT BRINGS OUT THE BEST IN PEOPLE

I have had numerous opportunities to work with families and family businesses that chose to put into writing what tools they wanted for bringing out people's best. The following is a list of the most commonly embraced values, with no one family or family business selecting more than six.

### The Golden Rule

"Treat others as you want to be treated." This is the most commonly selected. It calls for empathy as the point of reference for behavior. It has a universal appeal—for parents, for children, for customers, for employees, for people of any background.

### Honesty

The Ethics Resource Center of Washington, D.C., surveyed 4,035 employees at all levels working at companies of all sizes. Nearly one-third of those surveyed cited dishonesty as the most common kind of alleged misconduct at their companies: lying to supervisors, lying on reports, falsifying records, theft, altering product or service test results, and taking kickbacks.[4]

One of my clients defined honesty for their company this way:

"I will be truthful and fair in my dealings with customers, suppliers, and coworkers."

"I will keep my word."

"I will own up to my mistakes and pursue and take corrective action."

"I will provide feedback on things that don't look right to me."

I will never forget the family that valued honesty. Their engineer daughter had quit her good-paying job at a defense contractor after being forced to fudge her numbers on a government contract. Her family was proud of her for exercising a value they had stressed during her childhood—honesty. So they gladly took her back into the family home until she could find another job. Their pride increased a month later when they learned that Congress was going to investigate her former employer. Incidentally, she found a better job, and her former employee was found guilty of defrauding the government.

## Trustworthiness

This means you can count on the person. The person's word is good. A handshake seals the word. The person is not just out for self. You can count on him/her to know his/her stuff, to do the job, to follow through. The person will not undermine. The person works for the success of the family and company.

## Respect

Value is placed on other's ideas, skills, experience, beliefs, needs, feelings, suggestions, and rights. People are not discounted, or treated dismissively, or given the broad brush of baseless generalities.

## Knowledge/Learning

Emphasis is on learning. Learning via education, training, experience, reading, orientation programs, mentoring, continuing education, rehearsing, practicing, and benefiting from mistakes and risks taken.

I have never conducted a full-scale interview of employees for any company where I did not hear their desire for more training. I will never forget a big, burly man working for a family business getting choked up in front of his coworkers when he haltingly said to me during a group interview, "For eight years I've been stuck on the same machine. I ask them if I can train on the other machines. They say they need me on this one, and that there's no time. They don't care that I'm dead inside for forty hours a week." The group's silence was deafening. The business, incidentally, was sold within a year of this interview. The family could not lead their business any further.

It was beyond their management skill level. What they valued did not bring out the best in their people.

One further personal note on learning as a value. For eight years I was the master of ceremonies for my service club's tribute to the top sixteen graduating seniors of our two local high schools. The following groups year after year were overwhelmingly represented: Asians, Armenians, Jews, and Mormons. Invariably these outstanding young adults would say in their acceptance remarks to the audience, "I owe this honor to my parents. Education is something they insisted on for me and my brothers and sisters." Learning for these families is a family value.

### Work Ethic

A work ethic is learned at home and at school. Period. Children who do not have to lift a finger for their well-being, who have everything handed to them, and who are not required to fulfill their potential at each developmental stage grow up with an entitlement mentality.

### Responsibility

This is the number one motivator. Nothing motivates people like responsibility. People, whether little or big, are much more likely to excel when they are given responsibility for something from beginning to end. This is in contrast to simple obedience, where people, whether little or big, take no ownership for carrying through: "It's not my responsibility. I was just doing what I was told."

### Accountability

This has to do with consequences. Positive consequences for good performance: thank-yous, recognition, praise, and tangible rewards. Negative consequences for poor performers, nonperformers, and subtracting performers: the hot seat of explanation and learning for improvement, correction, coaching, goal setting, withholding of recognition and reward, or when all else fails, dismissal. In thirty years of experience working with families, I have concluded that accountability is the least practiced value of all. Parents, executive leaders, managers, and supervisors are simply reluctant to mete out consequences, either positive or negative.

## Cooperation/Interdependence

This proves to be very difficult for Americans. Children in many cultures have to learn cooperation beginning around their fourth year. But for American children, the rudimentary forms of cooperation learned early on collide with a culture that treasures individuality, self-reliance, the pioneering spirit, going it alone, looking out for yourself, and the prototype hero, the Lone Ranger. The "organizational man" of yesterday is being discredited during an era of down-sizing bureaucracies. In his place, businesses champion the entrepreneur, ending up out of necessity trying to do team building and create teamwork all over the place. The fact is that an enormous amount of work, both in families and in their businesses, requires cooperation and an appreciation of the interdependence of everyone and every role in order to get the job done.

## Excellence

To do something exceedingly well, up to "old world standards," is intrinsically rewarding. To do one's best paves the way to pride, pride in a good sense, and to increased self-confidence. Self-confidence cannot grow in a vacuum, or be mentally self-invented without accomplishment.

Excellence, however, must be distinguished from perfectionism, with its focus on the least little flaw. Perfectionism is a recipe for defeat. Like my cardiologist friend who pitched a no-hitter in Little League when he was eleven years old. He will never forget the stinging question of his perfectionistic father, who asked his son when he came bounding in the door with the news of his excellent performance, "How many did you walk?" Stung by his father's insensitivity, and perhaps jealousy, my friend felt defeated. (His father should've been at the game anyway!)

## Kindness/Compassion

This is a derivation of the Golden Rule. It is based on the old saying, "They don't care how much you know until they know how much you care." A simple act of kindness and compassion, when not done in a patronizing way, will always be rewarded by the grateful recipient. Two illustrations:

The founder of a family business bought a new, luxury sports car. The very first time he drove it in the driveway his six-year- old son came riding up on his bike. In his excitement about his dad's new car the boy drove right up beside the driver's window. The plastic handlebar grips were worn out, exposing the sharp ends. The handlebar ends gouged a long, deep streak through every layer of coating and paint along the driver's door. The boy instantly was afraid, and sad when he saw his father's anguished look. The dad got out of the car, reached out for his son, pulled him into a long hug and said, "I can always get a new car, but I only have one son." Compassion—and the boy has not messed with any of the three family vehicles since.

The second generation president of a family business was making his daily rounds of the factory, greeting people and asking how things were going. He noticed a middle-aged woman on the assembly line having to stoop over repeatedly to get parts and place them on a woefully low portable rack. He asked if she suffered from backaches. Shyly she acknowledged she did, but stated she was just glad to have a good job. Within the hour engineers and fabricators were getting her input for a newly designed parts rack. Kindness—she would go through fire for her president. The story spread throughout the plant almost as fast as gossip!

## Optimism

Children fed a diet of pessimism have little encouragement to dream dreams of an exciting future with them in it. They are not encouraged to excel for the goal of someday being important and valuable. The diet of pessimism goes like this: "That'll never work," "What's the use? It's just wishful thinking," "There will always be something," and "Life is just one damn thing after another."

Children who are taught that tomorrow will be worth living are encouraged to "go for it." They are taught the equivalent of the old saying, "Don't wonder how many seeds are in the apple. Wonder how many apples are in one seed." Their dreams and fantasies of

"when I grow up" are listened to with appreciation and encouragement. Founders of family businesses would be excellent role models
and "preachers" of optimism, given how they took huge risks on a
hunch that their idea or product will meet a successful tomorrow.
Family businesses are not for the faint of heart, or for the doomsayer.
They are for the optimists.

## Money as Morally Neutral

Money is neither intrinsically good nor bad. It is neutral. It
depends on how it is gotten and how it is used. It is a tool for good
or evil. Families can teach their children the value of money and its
potential for good from an early age.

The best example of this I have ever heard came from a private,
confidential conversation over lunch with a senior executive of a
multi-billion dollar, international family business. She was trying to
get across why the company was so successful, stressing how it was
partly due to the fact that this family over five generations wanted
their company to be driven by their family's values. She said, "It must
all go back to how they were raised. All their children from preschool
age on were given allowances with the following conditions: one-
third was to be saved, one-third could be spent freely, and one-third
had to be given to a good cause." This family's business is a household name the world over. Its generosity is just as legendary. Money
to them is something to be used to do good.

## Forgiveness

Mistakes, conflicts, hard feelings, and screw-ups are inevitable. At
home and at work. The vast majority of us feel guilty enough, even
before being confronted with the errors of our ways. And especially
so when we learn the effects on others of something we said or did.
Learning from these instances and making amends and corrections
for the future are crucially important. Equally important is getting a
fresh start, having the slate wiped clean. "When it's over, it's over."

The best in people is not brought out when there's no forgiveness. Learning, making amends and corrections, and making
commitments to a fresh start are impossible when peoples' pasts

are rubbed in their faces. People need to be let off the hook after turning around and going in a better direction.

Families and people in the workplace cannot grow without forgiveness. As the president of Physicians Sales and Services put it for his company, "We don't teach permission. That's a given. We teach forgiveness, so people will take risks and learn."5

## Fun/Laughter/Play

Enough cannot be said in praise of fun and laughter at home and at work. I discussed pleasure and enjoyment in the marriage and parenting sections above, claiming they are essentials of family best practices. It is equally true at work.

Southwest Airlines is notorious for its fun-filled skits, enjoyable flight crews, and goofy videos. The most productive company retreats I have facilitated have had generous amounts of time set aside for play. Breakthroughs in relationships and problems have occurred after the fun and games. I consulted at a company that has quarterly golf tournaments inside its two-story building. Golf consists of putting down corridors, under desks, down elevators, through the board-room—a two-story miniature golf course. Side bets and entry fees go to the company's favorite charity, a school they sponsor. Bragging rights are published repeatedly in the company's newsletter.

Fun, laughter, and play reduce stress, bring people closer together, remind everyone of our common humanity, and reduce the perceived size of problems to manageable proportions.

## HOW TO USE VALUES AS A TOOL

Once the family and its partners in the company have made explicit which five or so values they want as a compass for professional behavior, they are faced with a challenge. It is the challenge of making these values a very real daily influence.

The worst thing they can do is make a big deal out of having selected the values, and then never mention them again. The next worst thing would be to print them up and plaster them all over the place, and then never emphasize them again. Another worst practice would be to use the values as an advertising gimmick, claiming a "holier than thou" posture in the marketplace. Yet one more mistake: allowing a "gotcha" atmosphere to develop after the values have been chosen—"tah, tah, that's not being respectful", "well, that's not fair!", "rules violate our value of trust."

Companies that use values as tools to bring out the best in their partners employ a combination of many "indoctrination" strategies.

- They display the list of values prominently in many areas of the company, or, more discretely, give all employees personal copies for their workstations or to carry with them. Some companies do both.

- The top executive accepts personal responsibility for selling and teaching the values, doing so at every opportunity. It becomes part of his or her job description and performance review.

- Group discussions are held throughout the company to help everyone figure out how to apply the values to real-life work situations. These become on-going values/business ethics classes throughout the year.

- Recruitment of new hires from now on includes efforts to assess each candidate's "fit" with the values.

- Orientation for new hires (orientation for current employees is usually needed by most companies too) has a major and thorough emphasis on what the company stands for, how it wants its partners to treat customers and each other, and what it considers value-based, ethical behavior to be.

- A "value of the day" (or week, or month) is highlighted at team meetings, in in-house publications, and on displays, with application to work examples being the focus.

- Performance feedback, both formally written and informally spoken on an on-going basis, includes a section on conduct measured by values standards. This applies especially to leaders—anyone in a management, supervisory, or influential position. These employees are particularly looked to as role models. A portion of their bonuses and their chances for promotion are predicated on feedback from those reporting to them about how well the leaders lived the values. This is in keeping with a 1912 Scottish dictionary's definition of leadership—"going first by showing the way."

## SUMMARY

This chapter has implicitly addressed the fundamental question, "Can people be good?" I say yes. But never perfectly. But still yes. And I say people can be better when the bad side in all of us is discouraged and not tolerated. People can be better when the good side in all of us is taught, role modeled, required, expected, encouraged, and demanded. People can be better when the family and its business place priority on bringing out the best in people by using tools such as:

- The Golden Rule
- Honesty
- Trustworthiness
- Respect
- Knowledge/Know-how
- Work ethic
- Responsibility
- Accountability
- Kindness/compassion
- Cooperation/interdependence
- Excellence

- Optimism
- Money as a means to do good
- Forgiveness
- Fun, laughter, play.

These values, as well as others, are equally at home in families and family businesses. There is no difference, after all, between personal and professional values.

## BACK TO THE BASICS

Discuss with your family members and employees the following:

1. Which values from the above summary list do you already practice? Give examples.
2. Which values above do you wish you would practice? What difference would they make?
3. When have your values conflicted with the values of some customers or vendors?
4. What guidelines do you want followed when there is a conflict of values?
5. How can values be incorporated as attributes that are rated in performance feedback?
6. How can parents do a better job of instilling in their children any one of the following values: work ethic, responsibility, accountability, responsible money management?

## CHAPTER TWELVE

# Handy Household Hints on Communication

*One of the huge frustrations around here is our poor communica-tion. Dad isolates himself in his office. He relies on his secretary to tell us what he wants. And she in turn relies only on e-mail. Half the time our system is down anyway. In a company this size we don't need e-mail memos. We just need to talk. Person to person. But we don't. So we get this, "You should've known" malarkey. True, we should have known, but we didn't. Then we have this big brouhaha. Dad barks, my brother barks back, and the rest of us sit back, intimidated and amused. And after all this wasted energy and time, everything goes back to normal. Normal is surprises, not working things out, hard feelings, and fear of speaking up. It's easy to blame Dad, but the rest of us don't hold up our end of the bargain either. Rather than solving anything, we try to smooth everything over. Like I say, communication is a huge frustration around here.*

Tracy, age thirty-four, marketing,
civil engineering firm

WHEN FAMILIES AND EMPLOYEES IN FAMILY-OWNED businesses bring up the topic of communication, they all agree that it is the key to their success. They all mention the horror stories they have heard of family businesses going down the tubes because of a lack of communication or destructive communication. But like most families and most businesses, talking about communication is reminiscent of Mark Twain commenting on the weather: "Everyone talks about the weather, but no one does anything about it." This is somewhat unfair, however, because family businesses, like all businesses, try to do something to improve. They vow, first of all, to communicate better. Then they invest a lot of money in communication technology. Everyone ends up with a fax, cell phone, pager, voice mail, e-mail, Power Point presentation skills, and the promise of video conferencing some day. Sooner than later, however, most family businesses come face to face with a basic truth. In order to do something about communication, they must appreciate that there is no substitute for effective person-to-person communication.

Although high tech communication tools are helpful, it must be understood that the guts of business and of family life is person-to-person, face-to-face, live-and-in-color communication. Family and business are about relationships. The premise of these relationships is mutual success: "I want you to succeed, I want to succeed, I want us to succeed." Mutual success depends on people bringing out the best in each other. Effective person-to-person communication is one of the very best ways to do so.

But what is involved in effective communication anyway? Three important tools, at a minimum.

## THE TOP THREE COMMUNICATION TOOLS

In order to keep the topic of interpersonal communication manageable and practical, I have always limited my communications training programs to three basic tools—beliefs, careful listening, and straight talk. It has been my experience that family business people armed with these three tools can gain trust and respect, can convince and inspire, can bring up problems and solve problems, can create an environment of openness and accountability, and can stretch people without inappropriately stressing them. Beliefs, careful listening, and straight talk—three crucial communication tools for mutual success.

## Communication Beliefs

Strictly speaking, it is a stretch to call beliefs a communication tool. It is, however, helpful. Anyone holding negative beliefs about what makes people tick and the role communication plays in family and business relationships is destined to many unnecessary difficulties. Anyone holding positive beliefs about what makes people tick and the role communication plays has a genuine advantage. Negative beliefs build barriers, fuel bad feelings, harden positions, and prevent problem resolution. Positive beliefs build relationships, clarify feelings, promote clear thinking, and make problem solving possible. Beliefs make or break relationships, with communication the currency. Beliefs are one powerful communication tool.

### Negative Beliefs

Some people simply do not believe in the importance of communication. They do not believe in the need or importance of bringing out people's best. They believe that taking time to listen to someone is unnecessary. They believe in "tell 'em first," "let 'em have it," and "once you start listening you can't shut 'em up, so don't start in the first place."

Some people believe it is always best to say as little as possible. Choosing harmony over truth, they believe that sweeping things under the rug is best for the long run. Others believe that people only need to know "what they need to know." In business they believe it is management's role to mete out "what they need to know." In family life they believe in "what they don't know won't hurt them."

Many believe that people do not need to know how they are doing. They support our society's beliefs about compliments:

- "Don't compliment"—it goes to people's heads and they will slack off as a result
- "Don't compliment anyone above you"—it is apple-polishing, kissing up, and brownnosing

- "Don't compliment yourself"—it is bragging
- "Don't accept compliments"—it is better to turn down compliments and act undeserving
- "Don't ask for compliments"—it makes you look weak and desperate

Ironically, the same people who buy into the above nonsense are also reluctant to point out anyone's undesirable behavior or poor performance, especially at work: "I don't want to hurt their feelings."

Many do not believe in the benefits of honest, informed, open discussion. They believe it is better not to open things up, lest something cannot be quickly pushed through unchallenged, lest things get out of hand, or too much time is wasted. They grumble, "Communication is our number one problem. But it'll have to wait. We don't have the time. Are we going to sit around and talk about work, or are going to get something done around here?"

This is just a smattering of negative beliefs that undermine the best communication techniques. Far too many people just do not believe that the people who are the most respected, both at home and in business, are those who listen carefully and who talk straight. Whether they do so or not is largely a matter of what they believe.

## Positive Communication Beliefs

I have known people whose only communication tool was beliefs. These people were terrific communicators, without benefit of English as a first language, an education, a developed social vocabulary, or communication technology. Talking on the phone made them nervous, and they never could leave a message on an answering machine. But they cared about what others thought and felt. They did not beat around the bush. They connected with people because they wanted to. And they wanted to because they wanted to succeed and wanted others to succeed as well. To them, success was not a zero sum game.

The following are only a few communication beliefs that bring out the best in people. People do best . . .

when they know you want them to succeed;
when they are listened to;
when their needs and wants are understood;

when they are drawn out;

when they can safely get their feelings off their chest before being required to think first;

when their interests, needs, and wants are taken into consideration;

when they are dealt with straight;

when they achieve mutual understanding with others;

when they are kept informed;

when there are no surprises (except for celebrations);

when they are included from the start;

when they are invited to contribute;

when their ideas are required for creative innovation and improvements;

when they know how they are doing;

when they know how they stand with you;

when their performance and actions are corrected, not their personalities or motives;

when a negative situation is laid to rest—"when it's over, it's over";

when differences of viewpoint are respectfully encouraged;

when friendly humor is used;

when they live and work in a friendly atmosphere;

when they are not greeted with a problem right off the bat.

Fortunately there are people who approach their family members, employees, and customers with an "I want you to succeed, I want to succeed, I want us to succeed" approach. These people are well down the line as effective communicators. They would be so much more effective, however, were they skilled in the two arts of communication—careful listening and straight talk.[1]

### The Art of Careful Listening

It is an understatement to say that careful listening is an incredibly valuable communication tool for families and family businesses. That is like saying oxygen is key for family life and business. After all, how can family members be close at home, work effectively on the job, meet customers' needs, benefit from employees' suggestions and ideas, and solve problems without careful listening? The answer, of course, is that they cannot. Without listening there are no relationships that can truly succeed.

It is almost impossible to exaggerate people's need to be listened to. If given half a chance, people will unload, even to "frontline psychologists" like barbers and hairstylists, bartenders and neighbors, fellow workers and bosses. Some people even unload to total strangers—the guy on the next barstool, the woman on the airplane, the talk radio host. And some pay up to two hundred dollars an hour to be listened to by a professional listener in the helping professions. It is as though there were a law of nature, like the law of gravity. This law governs people's inner worlds: "What is inside people will come out." If what is inside does not come out in words and get listened to, it will come out eventually. It will come out in disturbed sleep, disturbed appetite, tension headaches, sore backs, nervous disorders. Or, it will come out in stressed behavior, broken relationships, empty relationships, violated relationships, or no relationships at all. Or, it will come out in management and employees alienated from each other, poor morale, ideas and suggestions for improvement lost, and problems mounting on top of more problems. Bottom line, we are built for communicating what we have inside. What we thus look for is someone who is willing to carefully listen to us, so our thoughts, feelings, wants, suggestions, needs, and hopes can come out safely. We instinctively do not open up to poor listeners.

### Two Types of Poor Listeners

There are two types of notoriously poor listeners that people recoil from or avoid altogether when they need to talk about something important. They are passive listeners and aggressive listeners, opposite

LISTENING CONTINUUM

| 1 | 5 | 10 |
| --- | --- | --- |
| Passive | Careful Listening | Aggressive |

ends of the listening continuum. Neither extreme listens carefully.

Passive listeners could be replaced by a tape recorder or a quiet dog. They just sit there and hear you, without listening. At home passive listeners keep reading the newspaper, looking at the television, and drinking their coffee while you are talking to them. At work they make furtive glances at their computer monitors, watch whomever goes past their open door, and continue to fiddle with paper clips and rubber bands. At meetings they are "out to lunch." Usually they can tell you what you have just said (proof they can hear), but clearly they are not listening, given their detached uninvolvement.

Any two-year-old child can tell when there is no careful listening going on. That is why a two year old climbs up on a nonlistening parent's lap, puts his or her hands on the parent's cheeks, pushes his or her nose hard against the parent's nose, and shouts to finally get through. By some gift of nature, people of all ages know the difference between hearing and careful listening.

Whether at home or at work, passive listeners send the message, "What you're saying, thinking, feeling, or needing is unimportant to me." The results are broken relationships. No one can get close to a passive listener at home or collaborate with a passive listener at work. And no one can solve problems with a passive listener, whether at home or at work, because he or she is simply too underinvolved.

Aggressive listeners break relationships too. They do not even hear a talker. The second they hear something they can talk about, or something they do not want to hear, or something they think they know better, or something they feel strongly about, they dive in and take over. Aggressive listeners also are "silence phobic." They will take over a conversation the second the talker pauses to take a breath or to collect thoughts. The arsenal of aggressive listeners includes interruptions, changing subjects, contradicting, correcting, voice raising, and protecting themselves behind a wall of words.

Whether at home or at work, aggressive listeners (actually they should not even be called listeners, since they do not listen at all) send the message, "What you are saying, thinking, feeling, wanting, or needing is unimportant to me." Sounds familiar—same message as the passive listener sends, only louder. And the results are the same too: broken relationships, because closeness at home, collaboration at work, and problem solving both places are impossible with someone who only wants to hear himself or herself talk.

### Careful Listening

What people need and want are careful listeners to talk with when they have something important to get across. Careful listeners are in the middle of the listening continuum. They combine what little is positive on each end of the listening continuum: the quietness of the passive end and the energetic involvement of the aggressive end. In order to talk openly, people need quietness, because they are searching around inside themselves to collect their thoughts, to find words to put to their feelings, and to sort out their issues in order to gain clarity. They also want a listener who is energetically involved, otherwise, they conclude, "what's the use?"

## LISTENING CONTINUUM

| I | 5 | 10 |
|---|---|---|
| Passive | Careful Listening | Aggressive |
| "hearing only" | | "talking only" |

There are four jobs a careful listener performs. These four jobs are based on the needs we all have when we have something important to get across.

***Let the story unfold.*** The first need is the need to tell our story. We look for some help to unfold our story completely. No one can talk the way we are taught to write an essay: an introduction, main points, summary, conclusion. The fact that we have to be taught to organize our thinking and feelings for writing is evidence enough that we need help getting our important stuff out. How often do we get interrupted before our story has unfolded, whether we are trying to explain ourselves to a customer service representative, to a supervisor, to a doctor or attorney, to a parent or spouse? How often do we start talking, only to get so far before coming to a premature ending? We have a lot more of our story to tell, but cannot think of anything more in that awkward moment. A careful listener helps the story unfold by

1. summarizing what has been said,
2. asking leading questions, and
3. inviting the talker to elaborate on what has been said or omitted.

With such help, the talker gratefully takes off again. A careful listener stays with a talker until the talker feels his or her story has finally unfolded: "Anything more before I respond?" Or, "Let's see if I got what you have all been saying." Careful listeners help the story unfold first, before responding. This is the first job of careful listening.

***Show understanding.*** The second need we have when communicating what is important to us is to be understood. Everyone wants to be understood. Everyone needs to be understood. Not being understood, or being misunderstood, does not bring out the best in anyone. It brings out frustration, confusion, anger, and loneliness. Being understood brings out satisfaction, confidence, clarity, a better sense of well being, and courage to continue relating to people important to us. A careful listener does better than saying "I understand." Most people hearing this cliché silently refute it anyway: "Like heck you do" or "You've never been in my shoes, so how would you know?" or "Don't patronize me." Instead of glibly saying, "I understand," a careful listener makes an observation about what is said that proves understanding. A careful listener shows understanding by

1. summarizing in other words what has been said,
2. giving a one or two sentence personal illustration of a similar experience, and
3. taking a guess at what the talker is feeling: "That must have been really frustrating" or "I bet that made you mad. I know it would me."

When a talker hears an accurate summary of what he or she has just said, only said in different words; when the talker hears that he or she shares some things in common with the listener; when the talker hears his or her feelings interpreted, the talker will in effect say, "I'm glad you understand." Because everyone needs and wants to be understood, a careful listener shows understanding. It is the second job of careful listening.

**Learn by listening.** The third need we all have when we have something important to say is to learn something about ourselves and about the person we are talking to. Frequently people will relate how, when carefully listened to, they discovered something about themselves, how the light bulb went on, how they did not realize they were already on the other side of a decision, or how strongly they felt about something. Frequently people will relate how, when carefully listened to, they learned how much the listener was interested, how much they had in common with the listener, how much the listener knew, how much the listener differed in viewpoint from the talker, or how much help the listener could or could not be.

This learning is of course mutual as well. A careful listener learns to appreciate a whole lot more about the talker than could otherwise be known. If you want people's ideas, suggestions, and cooperation, listen carefully to them. If you want to know how people feel about their work, their jobs, their careers, and what all motivates and demotivates them, just listen carefully to them. If you want to serve your customers and retain them by meeting their needs and customizing for them your services and products, listen to them carefully. If you want to know your children's aspirations regarding your family business, listen carefully to each one of them. If you want to learn how to be closer as a family, listen carefully to each of the members. There simply is no better way to learn important things about someone than to listen carefully to them. The third job then of careful listening promotes mutual learning.

***Respond with a conclusion.*** The fourth need we have when we have something important to say is the need to come to a conclusion. We do not bring out people's best when things just said are left hanging in midair. People get frustrated, disappointed, or ticked-off when they get no response to their sincere effort to communicate. If a listener has done an otherwise careful job of listening, but ends up walking away, hanging up, shrugging his or her shoulders, failing to commit to a course of action, either now or at a specified time in the future, the talker will not feel listened to, let alone carefully. Most likely the talker will avoid a repeat performance: "I'm not going in to talk to him anymore. It's no use. You don't get anywhere with him." Or, "Forget going to any more meetings. They say we should speak up. So we do. They listen. Sorta. And then zilch comes of it. It's a waste." Or, "I wish now that I hadn't opened up. I even cried in there. It was awful. I was left hanging. He could've at least said no, or set a follow-up time, or told me I was all wet. Something, at least. Never again."

Careful listeners prevent these futile experiences by taking it upon themselves to respond with a conclusion to the conversation. They approach an important conversation as though it were a funnel—wide open at the top of the conversation (who knows at first what the talker needs or wants to say?) and tapered down at the end to a conclusion. People want to get somewhere when they talk about things important. "Somewhere" can be as concrete as permission, an agreed upon course of action, a commitment to a future response, a no, a no for now, or a yes. Getting somewhere can also be less concrete. It can be simply, "I didn't know. Thank you for telling me." Or, "I'm as stumped as you. I gotta think this over. Let's talk again." Or, "That must've been tough. I hope you never have to go through something like that again." Or even, "I don't want to go over this stuff again. We're going in circles. Enough already." Virtually any response to what has been carefully listened to is better that no response at all. Talkers do not want to be left hanging. The fourth job of careful listening, then, is to respond with a conclusion.

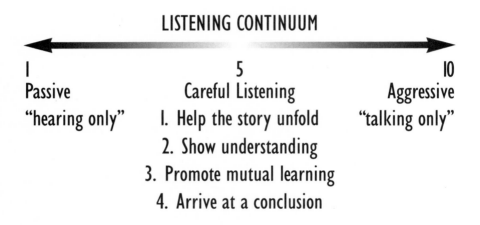

## LISTENING CONTINUUM

| 1 | 5 | 10 |
|---|---|---|
| Passive | Careful Listening | Aggressive |
| "hearing only" | 1. Help the story unfold | "talking only" |
| | 2. Show understanding | |
| | 3. Promote mutual learning | |
| | 4. Arrive at a conclusion | |

### Careful Listening Is Like Going Along for a Ride

In the hundreds of hours I have spent teaching careful listening skills to families, physicians, business executives, managers and supervisors, attorneys and judges in mediation training, and school principals, I have found the following analogy very helpful.

Think of careful listening as going along with the talker for a ride. For about the first 30 percent of the trip, **sit in the back seat** and simply ride along. The talker will drive the story wherever he or she wants or needs to go. When the talker comes to a dead end, help out with reminders that you are still along for the ride and interested in the scenery of the unfolding story:

- Comment briefly on what has interested you
- Make some noises of interest (oh, sure, huh, hmm, uh huh, really? no foolin? I'll be . . ., my gosh)
- Maintain frequent eye contact
- Look comfortable
- Repeat the last five words said

The talker will continue. Guaranteed.

When the talker's story has pretty much unfolded, ask to **sit up front in the passenger seat** as the conversation navigator. Careful listening from the passenger seat is usually 50 to 60 percent of the conversation. This is the heart of the conversation, where the real business of communication is conducted. The careful listener will . . .

- Summarize again what all has been heard
- Ask if it is time to ask some questions and make some comments
- Ask the talker to go over something again more slowly and thoroughly
- Ask the talker to go down a road not gone over to fill in the story
- Ask the talker to go another direction completely to learn the context of the talker's experience
- Comment on the talker's driving—his or her feelings
- Make observations about what the story must mean to the talker
- Summarize again "in other words"

When both talker and listener are satisfied that the story has unfolded, the talker feels understood, and both persons learned something, it is time for the listener to **get in the driver's seat** and drive the conversation home to a conclusion. The last 10 to 20

percent of the ride is the effort by both persons to reach a conclusion—an acceptable response by the listener especially, to prevent
the talker from feeling abandoned, stranded on his or her ride, or
compelled to go on and on with repetitions.

### Two Difficulties with Careful Listening

In my training experiences I have encountered two common difficulties people have in becoming more skillful listeners. One is the habit
aggressive listeners have of jumping into the driver's seat too early
(passive listeners never get in the car to even go on a ride). Sooner than
later they take over the trip by asking twenty-one questions. This does
not work well. The talker does not get the satisfaction of telling his or
her complete story. The questions can lead the talker on the listener's
trip, instead of the other way around. And conclusions reached simply
might not be right for the listener. The talker ends up feeling he or she
has not been carefully listened to.

The other difficulty is the fear that careful listening takes too long.
Actually, it the most efficient way to find out what a talker needs, wants,
thinks, or feels. It is like the old TV commercial for oil filters: pay a little
now, or pay a whole lot later. Again, the law of nature—if someone's
story does not come out now, it will come out eventually, usually in less
than beneficial ways. Careful listening can be done by skilled customer
service representatives on the phone in a couple of minutes. It can be
done by a carefully listening physician in ten minutes. It can be done at
work with a team meeting no longer than a half hour. It can be done in
the office with an employee in fifteen to twenty minutes. It can be done
between parent and child within fifteen minutes. It can be done
between spouses on a walk or over coffee on the patio. And with deep,
difficult matters, the fifty-minute "psychiatric hour" has proved over
the years to be sufficient to help people's story unfold, show them
understanding, promote mutual learning, and respond with conclusions. The efficiency of careful listening pays off both immediately and
later on. If they are not listened to now, people's stories will only
lengthen and their problems will compound.

## The Art of Straight Talk

Just as indispensable to quality communication as positive beliefs and careful listening are, so too is the art of straight talk. Without being talked to straight, people are left guessing about what people need and want to say.

How, for example, can a family member know what is expected of him or her in the family business if expectations have not been clearly laid out? How can a family member approach the family business constructively, if he or she does not understand the purpose, the values, the direction, and the goals of the family enterprise? How can a family member appropriately dream of a significant role in the business if he or she has not been told what is required of executive leadership, especially in terms of background preparation and job description? How can a family member find out he or she will not be part of the family business, if not told personally, directly, and carefully? How can a family member feel encouraged and grow in self-confidence, unless he or she is given personal, clear recognition?

It is no different at home. How can a spouse or child know they are appreciated, unless told in a straightforward manner? How can a spouse or child know what is needed of them, unless told? How can a spouse or child improve as a family member, unless their detracting and subtracting behavior are pointed out and alternatives discussed openly? How can a spouse or a child have their needs met, unless they speak up? How can family problems be resolved, unless everyone involved addresses the problem and offers their solutions? How can good feelings, like happiness and enthusiasm, lift a family? How can the meaning of hard feelings, like sadness, fear, and anger, be understood unless these feelings are verbalized clearly and constructively?

## The Opposites of Straight Talk

There are two types of talkers people struggle with. They are on the opposite ends of the talking continuum. People do not do well with passive talkers and aggressive talkers.

## TALKING CONTINUUM

I                                                                          10
Passive                                                          Aggressive

Passive talkers keep everyone guessing. They keep their ideas, feelings, wants, and needs locked up inside. They sit there either all bottled up, play the sympathy game of shyness, or deliberately withhold their say to keep everyone at arm's length. They hide behind the little pronoun *me:* "Don't ask me." Or, "It doesn't matter to me." Or, "It's not up to me." Or, "Don't look to me for that." Or, "Don't expect me to step forward." Or, "Why do you want me for that?" Or, "Why does this always happen to me?"

Even though passive talkers try to smooth everything over to keep things harmonious, they are seldom respected. Why? No one can get very close to them at home, or team up with them at work. They contribute too little. No one can solve problems with them, whether at home or at work. They would rather deny a problem exists. They go their own comfortable way by sweeping things under the rug. No one can be himself or herself around them. They do not believe in honesty and the biblical value that "you shall know the truth, and the truth shall set you free."[2] Passive talkers do not bring out the best in people, let alone themselves.

The other side of the talking continuum is equally problematic. Aggressive talkers keep everyone at arm's length too, only they use bludgeoning report cards. They are very free with their judgments and opinions. To them anyone and anything are free game for evaluation. They overuse the big pronoun *you* in handing down their judgments: "The trouble with *you* is, and *you* know damn well *you* do this. *You* always are doing that and *you* never once get it right.

Where do *you* get your approach, anyway? *You* are just like all the rest of *you* all. *You* are no different. I'll tell *you* right now, and *you* get this right, *you* hear me, *you* will never again . . . And *you* look at me when I'm talking to *you*!"

Aggressive talkers are even more self-righteous than passive talkers. Whereas passive talkers feel guiltless for not saying anything (which is of course the problem), aggressive talkers are reinforced by our cultural icons: movie characters who verbally and physically blow people away, Patton-type military heroes, football coaches screaming on the sidelines, "chainsaw" executives who cut through their corporations, and pop psychology that encourages victims to really open up. Aggressive talkers also feel very righteous because our culture sanctions such phrases as "smash mouth," "in your face," "let 'em have it point-blank right between the eyes," "give 'em hell, by God," "give 'em the old woodshed treatment," "go ahead and have a come-to-Jesus meeting with 'em, they deserved it," or "you at least know where you stand with the bugger, even if you've been cut to size."

Although aggressive talkers try to be honest, and usually can go forward "like nothing happened" (trouble is, something did happen and usually it was not very constructive), they are seldom completely respected. Why? For the very reasons passive talkers are not respected. Same results, only louder. No one can get very close to them at home or team up with them at work. No one knows when they will get their heads bit off. No one can solve problems with them, whether at home or at work. No one can be himself or herself around them. Their hammerlike bluntness inhibits expression and behavior. Aggressive talkers with their report cards do not bring out the best in people, let alone themselves.

## Straight Talkers

People do best with persons who talk straight. People respond well to someone who has an ease of style, as passive talkers have, and the energy and involvement of aggressive talkers. Straight talkers are in the middle of the talking continuum.

## TALKING CONTINUUM

| 1 | 5 | 10 |
| :--- | :---: | ---: |
| Passive | Straight Talk | Aggressive |
| "me" | | "YOU!" |

Straight talkers do not beat around the bush, or elbow their way to dominance. They avoid the mushy passive jargon of the helping professions: the "sorta, kinda, maybe, try, perhaps if we could possibly" beat-around-the-bush words that rob people and language of potency. And they avoid the offensiveness of the aggressive. Straight talkers speak for themselves, about themselves.

Straight talkers are clear about what they think, what they want, what they need, what they feel, what they are willing to do. Straight talkers say yes and say no with thought and forthrightness. They get to the point, without stepping on anyone. When they finish talking, everyone is clear about the talker's position, without feeling disrespected in the process.

Here are some straight talk examples:

*Our customer was very happy to get that order in such a short time. I appreciate you going the extra mile. Nice job. Thanks.*

*I hate to rain on the parade here, but I am in disagreement about going ahead with this project. I don't think we've done adequate market research. We have no solid cost projections. And the people who are going to have to shoulder it all are already overloaded. I am going to vote no.*

*Ladies and gentlemen. Although it is eleven months until next Christmas, I am already announcing that the money we just spent on the $300 gift certificates for every one of us will be given to charity next year. Your gift committee was as diligent as they could be in spending the $16,000 the company gave to say "Merry*

*Christmas." But I have a sour taste in my mouth after hearing so many people grumble and complain about the certificates being from the wrong store, being too cheap, being taken away from wages, and so on. I am disappointed. This lack of gratitude violates our values of respect and courtesy. I am open anytime to anyone who will help me learn from this. Maybe I or we are doing something wrong across the board. I don't know. But until I find out, I remain disappointed and committed to a nice gift to charity next Christmas in our company's name.*

*Son, I want you to succeed. And I want our family's business to succeed. That's why I have decided to delay your promotion to the presidency. I have decided to hire someone from the outside who has national experience. I want you to take over our distribution division. It is the one area you haven't conquered yet. It's underperforming and needs your high-tech skills badly. It would give you the experience I think you need. I have given this a lot of thought. I have gone over it with the board and your mother. I can imagine that this is disappointing to you. So much so that you don't have to respond right now. I'd like to get your thoughts and feelings on this tomorrow. Sleep on it and we'll talk. But know this—my decision is final.*

*Daughter, I am going to bring up something unpleasant. I want to find out your perspective on something. My secretary has been with me, as you know, almost as long as you have been alive. She has been wonderful. But ever since you came on board earlier this year, her mood and performance have gone south. And this morning I overheard the two of you exchange some pretty tough stuff. I don't like it. It's not O.K. with me to have two key players around here having interpersonal problems. And you know me. I refuse to let anything be swept under the rug. So help me understand, from your end of things. I intend to talk to her also, right after she gets back from lunch.*

*If I could have my way on our vacation, I would like for it to be just the two of us. Many parents, I'm sure, would love to have a family vacation. But I want you all to myself, and I need a break from the kids. It would be a vacation for them at grandma's and grandpa's anyway. I want us to rent a furnished condo on the beach. We can do some gourmet cooking together like we used to, and we can take long, long walks on the beach. I want to sleep late every morning. I want to read two books. And I want to drive the cart while you golf everyday. I don't want to ruin my vacation trying to work on my thirty-five handicap. This is what I want. Your turn—I want to hear what you want to do.*

*I don't want to be confronted the first minute I walk in the door with all the things the kids did and didn't do. I hate this role of being the heavy right off the bat. Let me at least go in and change and first monkey around with the kids a little bit. I know this sounds like all I want to be is a fun-time parent. But criminy, I don't want to be an enforcer before I can enjoy you and the kids. And I won't be an enforcer for stuff that happened when I wasn't here. Unless it's something huge. Let's talk this over after we get them to bed. Will you sit down with me later so we can figure something out?*

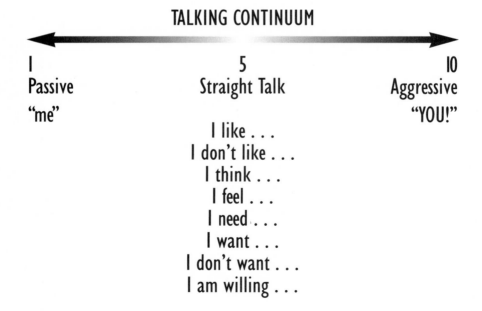

## TALKING CONTINUUM

| 1 | 5 | 10 |
|---|---|---|
| Passive | Straight Talk | Aggressive |
| "me" | | "YOU!" |

I like . . .
I don't like . . .
I think . . .
I feel . . .
I need . . .
I want . . .
I don't want . . .
I am willing . . .

## A Common Difficulty

A common difficulty in straight-talk training is people's fear. A lot of people are afraid of hurting someone's feelings by talking straight. This fear inhibits them from saying what they need to say. I have given several responses over the years concerning this fear of hurting someone by talking straight.

First, straight talk does not include character judgments, name calling, evaluations of lineage, or any other types of disrespect. People are not violated or discounted by straight talk. True, straight talk at times involves report cards. But it is done to assist the person to better succeed. Straight talk focuses on undesirable behavior and necessary corrections, not on the person's character. Second, people do at times feel badly when they are given straight news. But it is important to avoid the "he who wrings the hanky rules the world" baloney. People's momentary feelings cannot hold hostage the long-term benefits of problem solving that the combination of straight talk and careful listening can provide. Third, it is best to deal with problems now, rather than allow the problems to grow into mountains that are truly scary to climb. Lastly, straight talk is also very much about positives—telling others straight out how much you love them, appreciate them, want them, and want them to succeed.

People who talk straight bring out the best in people. They end up respected as well.

## SUMMARY

People who are good to live with, work with, and do business with . . .

- Believe in what effective communication can do for them
- Believe in what effective communication can do for others
- Value what they have inside them
- Value what others have inside them as well

Consequently, they . . .

- Carefully listen—they help people tell their whole story, show them they are understood, help them learn about themselves, and help them come to conclusions
- Talk straight—they respectfully let others know what they think, feel, like, want, need, and are willing to do

### BACK TO THE BASICS

Have separate meetings with your family and your employees to address the following:

1. List five recent examples of good communication. What beliefs about people and communication do these examples reveal?
2. List three recent examples of communication breakdown. What beliefs about people and communication do these examples reveal?

On your own:

1. Select someone with whom you have been meaning to have a conversation. Your goal is to carefully listen. Remain mostly quiet for at least ten minutes. Prove to him or her that you understand what has been said. Be sure to summarize what you have heard. Together arrive at a conclusion, including "let's do this again."
2. Say thank you and pay compliments at least three times a day. After a month, consider what difference this straight talk has made.
3. Select someone with whom you need a heart-to-heart talk. Prepare and rehearse ahead of time your main points, being sure that you will be speaking about your positions, your reactions, and the other's actions, not personality. Have the meeting. Once you have finished your straight talk, sit back and listen, without interruption, to the other's response. Summarize what you have heard. Agree to meet again as soon as possible to discuss a plan of correction.

## CHAPTER THIRTEEN

# Why Have Family Meetings?

*I had heard of other family businesses having family meetings. It sounded good to me. So I rented a room at a lakeside resort, invited our CPA and attorney, and told the two boys we would meet all day Saturday to go over year-end things and make some plans for next year. I'm telling you, it was a disaster. We were out of there by noon. That was a year and a half ago, and we still haven't brought it up. It's like a five-ton elephant sitting in the middle of the room, and no one will mention it. My one son, no sooner than we got started, started in on his brother. Then on me. It was like he was waiting for the moment to let loose with everything he had bottled up. Things were said back and forth that will never be forgotten. Or maybe even forgiven. So much for family meetings.*

Anonymous

MEETINGS ACROSS THE BUSINESS LANDSCAPE HAVE A poor reputation. And deservedly so. They are often too long and unproductive. They cost a lot, given everyone's salary while they are sitting there. They waste the time of most of those attending because they focus on issues involving a few. People often do not know the purpose of the meeting, do not know what is expected of them, come unprepared, sit there disengaged, speak up to either look good or keep quiet to look good, and cannot wait to be called out for something "urgent."

And seldom are meetings conducted by someone skilled enough to help the participants achieve what only a collective effort can achieve: results that are greater than the sum of individual thinking.

## MEETINGS ARE IMPORTANT

Meetings are in fact critical to the life of any business, including family businesses. Business today does not resemble the medieval crafts guilds of individual artisans working solo. Business is now a complex of workers interrelated and interdependent like never before, especially since it is so crucial to be efficient and cost effective. The coordination to increase efficiency calls for meetings. The mix of thoughts, ideas, expertise, experience, wants, and needs of the participants can produce results that no one person can come up with alone. Cross-fertilization of thinking stimulates new thinking, breakthrough ideas, collective responsibility, and shared commitments—things not able to be achieved another way. People in the meeting room have "got it" individually, but it takes an effective meeting with others to bring "it" out.

Meetings are like good cooking: mixing and blending all the individual ingredients and then applying some heat. The results are something far greater and beneficial than any one raw ingredient alone can contribute. Meetings are like good music: mixing and blending all the voices of individual instruments into a fuller, richer sound than any solo can produce. It is as though 2+2=5 after both 2s are really mixed, blended, and heated together.

Business people intuitively realize all this. That is why so many meetings are called. And families owning businesses intuitively realize this as well, especially when it comes to family matters in business. Some of the most important family topics that family business people need to address are ownership issues. They are the responsibility of the family itself. These ownership issues are best dealt with at family meetings, where the family and its business can be more positively influenced than any one of them can accomplish alone.

## THE WAYS FAMILIES CAN MEET

There are informal and formal ways families can meet to address their ownership issues. Both are valuable.

### Informal Meetings

There are family owners who meet with each other on an informal basis because they believe in keeping each other informed, believe three, four, and five heads are better than one or two, and believe that everyone should be on the same page. These families in effect say, "We're all in on this together, so let's act like it and talk about it together."

Their founder, for example, invites the adult children over for dinner to discuss what is on his or her mind, or to find out what is on theirs. He phones children who do not live in the area, relating to each of them the same message, or sounding each out on a particular issue. A second generation leader can do the same with siblings and nieces and nephews who are of age. Some families take vacations together and reserve a time to discuss business: when everyone realizes that this is an important part of the vacation, and when business discussion is confined to a set time, without washing over into relaxation and fun time, these meetings can be important. When news needs to be shared that every owner deserves to hear, informal contact is good: this keeps everyone in the know. I know a family that reserves the day after Christmas for an informal owners meeting. Grandchildren and the family dog are included as the adults go over year-end highlights, open dividend gifts (in family business, dividends are gifts), and casually discuss the year ahead.

These informal owners meetings are very influential. They set the tone for how family owners get along with each other, especially the relations between those who work inside the business and those who do not. When their informal meetings are handled openly, in a civil, friendly manner, and careful listening and straight talk are practiced, they pave the way for having more successful formal meetings in the future. The opposite, of course, is equally true. When there is garbage from past informal meetings, the more formal meetings have an uphill climb from the very start.

### Formal Meetings

There are ownership issues that are simply too crucial and too complex to be left to informal meetings. These include the distinction between ownership and management, ownership benefits, ownership succession, family members' employment in the business, the purpose of the family and of the business, the values for guiding the company, business education, management succession, contingency management succession, and the family's response to a crisis or an emergency in the business. These issues are discussed in greater detail below. These complex issues are at the very heart of what it means to be in a family business. They require disciplined, well thought out, well run meetings.

Small families, which typically include those that are still in their first and second generations, can hold formal meetings that are attended by all family members of age, meaning grandchildren in their middle to late teens. These families at times also have legitimate reasons to include only their own children; meeting without sons-in-law, daughters-in-law, and grandchildren sometimes helps the family stay better focused on the issues.

Larger families and those into the third generation and beyond cannot conduct meetings on ownership issues very effectively or efficiently if the meetings are attended by thirty or more people. Some families would have well over a hundred people if all were invited. The vast majority of these second and third cousins are considerably removed from the business, let alone from each other. These families do not feel like "family" anyway. Connections are not nearly so emotional as they are material. Since there are too many owners for a "town hall meeting," and family interests are mostly business and ownership issues, these families would do well to establish what could be called a Family Council, or Ownership Group, or Board of Owners.

A Family Council would be made up of nine to twelve owners representing several generations. It would be best if they were either elected at large by all owners, or from nominees selected by a small group of owners acting as a selection or nominating committee.

This Family Council would have several responsibilities. Its representatives would decide the key ownership issues. They would inform, explain, and interpret their decisions to the rest of the owners. They would select family members and outside, independent experts to the company's board of directors (see chapter 14). They would be the boss of the board of directors, because they represent shareholding owners and family investors. They would act as the liaison between the board of directors and the rest of the family. And they would be responsible for educating the teenagers and young adults of the family about the history and status of the business, the ownership arrangements in place, the values of the business, the requirements of employment in the business, the direction and goals the company is currently pursuing. The Council would also encourage the young adults to have their own hopes and dreams for the business, and to express them to the Family Council.

Families that hold both informal and formal meetings of owners take their family's business for what it is. It is serious business. There is a lot at stake. Nothing should be left to chance, or to assumptions.

## THE NUTS AND BOLTS OF FAMILY MEETINGS

Before addressing the five ownership issues that require the work of family meetings, it would be best to first discuss the nuts and bolts of family meetings. Many families know it would be a good idea to meet together but do not know how to really go about it. Others have heard horror stories of family meetings blowing up and want to avoid this happening to them. And others have tried but were not satisfied with the results. Fortunately there are families that have very successful family meetings. Their meetings have become regular events, whether annually, biannually, or quarterly. What these families do so effectively is worth emulating, especially the rules they use for guidance and assurance.

**Family Meeting Rules**

The chances of having successful family meetings are greatly enhanced when everyone beforehand understands how the game is played. This is only common sense. Why ad-lib something so important? Why cause family members anxiety by keeping them guessing about what is going to happen and what is expected of them? Why try to bring out the best in each family member during the meeting without the benefits of some sensible structure?

A couple of family members, if not the founder or head of the business, first need to poll everyone for their suggestions on how they prefer the meeting to be, and for issues and questions they would like addressed. This already begins a collaborative effort and avoids people feeling something is going to happen to them, rather than with them. Issues about the when, where, and who of the family meeting can also be handled at this time.

Families who have had successful family meetings usually come up with variations on the following general rules:

1. Everyone is to receive in writing, at least two weeks in advance, the purpose, the agenda, and the expected results of the family meeting.
2. No one is to cook up outcomes or politic privately with other attendees before the meeting.
3. Everyone is asked to come prepared. Background information, articles, and books important to the meeting's subject matter should be distributed two weeks in advance as well: "Come with an open mind and a sense of humor. Read the enclosed material. Have your thinking organized and questions ready to go. This will be a good meeting."
4. Everyone is to cooperate with the facilitator of the meeting. The facilitator needs to be someone who is neutral, trusted, and respected by all family members. The facilitator also needs to be someone skilled at conducting meetings. The facilitator can be a family member, preferably someone not working in the family's business, or can be an outsider. It is seldom a good idea to have someone as

powerful as a parent conducting the meeting. Family members will be more involved and expressive when the parents are "fellow travelers."

5. Starting times and finishing times are to be observed. Starting late sets a tone that is too easygoing. And any meeting expands to the time allotted. Better to allow the clock to push concentration for results. Allow generous times for breaks; efficiency drops after 90 minutes, if that long, for some people. Diminishing returns and less than positive behaviors tend to occur when people are pushed beyond their energy levels.

6. Everyone is expected to participate. Period.

7. Everyone is to stay on topic. And each topic raised should be completed as much as possible to prevent loose ends and the frustration of not accomplishing much. "War stories" and illustrations should be mostly limited to the more relaxed times, like breaks and meal times.

8. No one is to be interrupted during the meeting, except for genuine emergencies. Family members are too important to a family meeting to be distracted or pulled away.

9. Every decision made is to be written down, including the following: mutually agreed upon wording of decisions, who is responsible, what the time frame is, how the decisions will be communicated to those impacted, how they will be measured, and how everyone in the family will know the outcomes of the decisions.

10. The time and purpose of the next meeting is to be mutually agreed upon. Just as the family's business is ongoing, so too should family meetings. They are too crucial to be a one-shot deal or a sometime thing.

These general meeting rules are usually augmented by some basic communication rules:

1. Everyone has a say.
2. Everyone has a turn.

3. Everyone listens carefully.

4. Everyone proves he or she understands before going any further.

5. Everyone is expected to ask questions, for clarification or for information.

6. No one interrupts anyone.

7. No one brings up the past to discredit anyone.

8 No one gives report cards on anyone's personality or character.

9. No one gives up or checks out when the going gets tough.

10 No one keeps the meeting going privately when not in session.

11. Everyone remembers that friendly humor is the shortest distance between people.

12. Everyone proves before adjournment that there is mutual understanding on all decisions made.

## Handling Emotional Issues and Controversy

It is inevitable that every family owning a business will face an actual or brewing emotional issue or controversy that involves the entire family. And as families mature and expand over the years, there are the inevitable, difficult crossroads to be negotiated. Resolving these emotional issues, diffusing the controversies, and negotiating these crossroads require the "2+2=5" collective wisdom that effective meetings can generate.

These difficulties need to be dealt with before anything else is addressed. Family meetings should not be held in the mistaken hope that these difficulties can be ignored. They will cloud over all other issues and, more than likely, will erupt in a charged family setting. Besides, no family member can be expected at a meeting to think clearly and contribute to fair and creative problem solving if he or she is fearful, hurt, angry, or confused. No family or family member experiencing turmoil can abide by the best laid agenda and meeting rules. These feelings have to be expressed safely, fully understood, and channeled into constructive energy before a formal family meeting is held.

It is at this point that a neutral, outside professional facilitator who understands families and family businesses can be invaluable. This facilitator can interview each family member, including spouses and children of age. In private. Confidentially. Everyone can thus speak freely and express in not so careful ways all the emotional issues. Potentially damaging communication can be defused. Everyone can finally feel understood. Once unburdened of raw emotion and feeling understood, family members can begin thinking constructively.

Usually a facilitator will find common themes that have emerged from the individual, private interviews. And many positive things will have been expressed that have never been spoken openly to the family.

Armed with these themes and positives, a facilitator can return to each family member privately to begin preparing everyone for the family meeting they have all been dreading, but have known intuitively they need to have.

This charged family meeting is best conducted by the facilitator who interviewed everyone. The facilitator will have gained everyone's trust and confidence, and in all likelihood will be the point person during the meeting for enforcing needed communication rules, for creating a safe atmosphere for constructive openness, for keeping things focused, for preventing things from getting out of hand, for keeping the family from reverting back to old habits, and for steering the group hard toward needed resolutions.

The risks of avoiding such a family meeting are enormous. The risks are equally enormous when the family meeting is carelessly handled. Almost all families, when given a fair chance to resolve their emotional issues and controversies, and given a chance to negotiate the inevitable crossroads of family business life, will discover the good qualities and goodwill of each family member. Although it is disguised in many ways, and by many mistakes along the way, blood is thicker than water and money. Sometimes it takes a major breakthrough family meeting to discover this again.

### Selecting Outside Help

It has been suggested several times that a family business consultant can be helpful. This is especially true when the family needs to address difficult emotional issues, when the family is inexperienced with family meetings, when the family is at the threshold of a generational change in ownership and/or management, and when the family is struggling with unsatisfactory results at home and/or at work. Trying to go it alone on issues such as these is worse than trying to give yourself a haircut—there is a lot of stuff you just cannot see.

It is rare for the family's attorney, accountant, or banker to work beyond their fields of expertise and training. The best and most professional among them become confidants to the family who encourage their clients to add a family business consultant to the team when emotional and controversial issues are present. Often their endorsement of a family business consultant is sufficient for the family to entrust themselves to a new source of help.

When a referral is not this convenient, families would do well to trust a "word of mouth" referral from other family business people they know and trust. A consultant should be:

- Trustworthy
- Honest
- Educated and experienced in working with families
- Experienced in the business world
- Skilled in communication
- Levelheaded with common sense
- Capable of neutrality
- Capable of effectively saying what needs to be said
- Professional with the issue of confidentiality

Upon receiving favorable information, a family can proceed with some confidence. If no "word of mouth" candidate is apparent, the family could attend family business conferences to evaluate presenters, or contact university business schools for possible referrals.

In all cases, however, the family, at least the key decision makers, should always personally interview a potential candidate. The first job of the interview needs to be about "fit." Always hire for "fit." If a consultant does not fit into the family's style, or has a personality uncomfortable to the family, it would be best to look elsewhere.

The second job of the interview is to gain satisfactory answers to the following questions:

1. What is your experience working with families, especially family matters like relationships, emotional issues, different generational needs, and communication? What is your training in family studies? How many families have you worked with? Over how long a time? And are you a parent yourself?

2. What is your experience in the business world, especially regarding management issues, leadership, employee relations, and the role of a board of directors? What types of businesses have you specialized in, and at what stages of the corporate life cycle do you have the most experience?

3. How do you approach your work with a family business? And how do you gain everyone's trust?

4. How do you handle information told only to you? How do you remain neutral?

5. How do you approach sensitive, emotional, potentially volatile issues?

6. How do you facilitate family meetings? What are your rules?

7. Tell us about your most successful experience.

8. Tell us about your most disappointing result. What did you and the family learn from this?

9. What do you do when things do not go well, and some family members want to quit this process?

10. What should we expect from beginning to end as we go forward? What potential problems could arise?

11. How long does this process last? Do you do follow-ups and follow-throughs?

12. How will we know when we no longer need your services?

13. How easy is it for you to say "I don't know"?

14. What are your fees? For what do you charge and not charge?

15. How will you bill us?

16. How available are you? Do you charge for phone calls?

## FIVE OWNERSHIP ISSUES

Once fortified by constructive guidelines on how to approach family meetings, families need to get together to address ownership issues. These are distinct from the day-to-day management issues inside the company. Ownership issues are the sole province of the owners. A family business cannot succeed for long, let alone from one generation to the next, with uninformed, uninvolved, or misguided owners. Family meetings are called for in order to help family members become good owners.

### Ownership and Management Are Different

Too often families equate ownership and management. It is understandable. We are taught from childhood that when we own something, we take care of it. And taking care of it means hands-on "management." Personal possessions, however, and the family business do not equate. This distinction must be a repeated theme taught in the home by parents in informal ways throughout their children's lives:

> *Yes, our name is on the sign. This is our business. We have a lot of people who do not belong to our family who work here. They know how to work here. They want to work here. Someday, if you want to work here, and learn how at school and by first working at other places, you can work here too. But you don't have to. Our name will still be on the sign if you work here or not. We're the owners.*

This theme is further made clear at family meetings. It is more of a theme than an agenda item, unless the family has unfortunately been remiss on this issue during the children's younger years. If this is the case, then a whole meeting should be focused on this distinction. Why? First of all, it is a business reality. The genius of capitalism has long separated ownership and management; witness the role of stock markets in publicly owned companies. Making a family business analogous to this reality is a good lesson taught. Families also do not want their children feeling either entitled to employment or obligated to be employed at the family's business. When children of age attend family meetings and listen to discussions centered on ownership issues, they learn again the distinctions:

- Ownership is by birth; management is by competency
- Ownership is given; management is earned
- Ownership is from love; management is from education, training, experience, and performance
- Ownership is who you are; management is what you do
- Ownership is about the big picture; management is implementing the big picture
- Ownership is about doing the right things; management is about doing things right
- Ownership is about the purpose and values of the business; management is about day-to-day execution of the purpose and values
- Ownership serves the business's needs; management fulfills the needs
- Ownership is about distribution of earnings, shareholding, and estate planning; management is about salaries, compensation, and performance incentives

For some families, the above ownership distinctions are overdrawn. These families equate ownership and merit. They make it clear, sometimes belatedly, that a wayward child who has brought shame to the family, or has an intractable case of irresponsibility, in effect "disowns" himself or herself from owning a piece of the family's business. This depends on the family's values and sense of accountability.

Two notes of caution, however. Eventual ownership should not be used as a manipulative tool by parents in an effort to get childlike obedience from an adult child. Why have a kid comply with parents' wishes just for the money? Money is hardly a healthy motivator inside a family. Also, denying ownership sometimes should not be punishment for a child who did not work out as an employee in the family's business. It is one thing if the child blatantly performed in self-sabotaging, self-defeating ways. But it is another if the child was misguided in working for the family's business in the first place. The family itself shoulders some of the responsibility for this as well. A child should not be disowned from the family business because he or she was the wrong person in the wrong position in the wrong line of work in the wrong company. Thus the conditions of ownership, if beyond family membership, are issues that need to be addressed at family meetings.

Families that have been consistently addressing the distinctions between ownership and management in both informal and formal ways have an advantage. They will have less confusion and conflict. Ownership benefits, ownership succession, employment at the family's business, and management succession are clear, thanks to effective family meetings.

### What's Our Purpose?

It is easy to assume that everyone in the family understands the purpose of the family and the purpose of the business simply by observation and experience over the years. Assumptions, unfortunately, can easily lead to family members being at cross purposes with each other during times of stress. Family meetings can be the ounce of prevention ahead of time that addresses the issue of purpose.

### Purpose of the Family

Families benefit greatly when they gather all generations together and formally discuss their purpose as a family. It can be a very reassuring experience for everyone. Elders can begin the meeting with family history and "tribal stories" that richly contribute to everyone's sense of belonging. Humble beginnings recalled and repeated yet again can remind everyone of the fragile nature of success. Risks taken, sacrifices made, mistakes made, victories achieved, and hopes yet to be met become lessons for the future. Parents can reiterate how irrationally committed they have been to each of their children, and now to their children's own families. This parental love in equal proportion for each family member can balance the normal and ever present feelings of sibling rivalry.

Children and grandchildren need to talk at these family meetings too. Each is encouraged to share hopes, dreams, goals, plans, and needs. Encouraged too can be fears, disappointments, differences, and even dislikes. Amid the laughter, grins, knowing winks and nods, and sometimes tears, emerge the feelings of being accepted, understood, and supported that family members can experience only in a family setting.

The family member most gifted with words and courage can articulate a "rough draft" of the family's purpose. For example,

> Our family, our ties, our love are more important than money, position, and past hurts. We'll help each other, if asked. We're family. And no one, not even any of us, should ever try to rob us of this.

Romantic, too idealistic, too touchy-feely? No, just the honest work of family love. Work that even the toughest and most hard-boiled families are willing to do if the family meeting is approached constructively. Family meetings like these can bless everyone.

### Purpose of the Business

These family meetings can also focus on the owners' purpose for the business. Families need to articulate a compelling, unifying business purpose such as those discussed in chapter 3. They also need to articulate the business values that guide all employees, discussed in chapter 10.

Additionally, the family needs to make explicit whether the business is dedicated to short-term or long-term success. For example, the owners together can decide that the purpose of the business is to primarily provide for long-term financial security for future generations. This purpose, then, guides decisions regarding current distributions, long-term capital expenditures, investments, estate planning, and, of course, management direction.

Family meetings about the business purpose are also forums to decide the question of employment of family members in their business: "Is the purpose of our business to provide careers for current and future generations? If so, what are the rules? What education, training, outside experience and success, competencies, and passions are required of any of us to work in our own company?" When the parents put forth their rules, and children contribute their views, the family takes a proactive and positive step toward management succession in the future.

Discussion at these family meetings can also clarify the civic and charitable roles that the family and the business will play in the community.

## Business Education

No family business can succeed much beyond the average twenty-four years life expectancy for family businesses if its owners do not know how to think like business persons. Family meetings, annually at a minimum, are needed by all family members for basic business education. Topics to be covered include the company's core competencies, the customer base, customer responses to satisfaction surveys, the market potential, the industry, the competition, and the local, national, and global economies. Family members also need to know the highlights and shortcomings of the past year, and the opportunities and risks of the next. A good basic understanding of the financial scorecard, both year-end results and status of ownership assets, is needed by everyone. This necessitates the use of meaningful bar graphs, trend lines, and pie charts, rather than complex accounting spread sheets. Performance evaluations of key personnel and goals for the coming year are also appropriate, especially for families acting more or less as a board of directors.

The purposes of these straightforward business education meetings are to inform, clear up unspoken assumptions, and make sure everyone is on the same page. Family owners can then better discuss ownership issues and make decisions with business sense. The meetings are also an excellent forum for grooming the next generation to think strategically and responsibly about their future roles.

It is best to strictly limit these educational meetings to an informational agenda. These meetings are for learning and thinking, both of which are diminished when emotional issues are addressed at the same time. Emotional issues are to be dealt with at other family meetings, like those discussed above.

## Three Types of Succession Planning

The most often discussed issue at family business conferences is succession planning. Admittedly, it is crucially important, but it is not something families have to deal with day in and day out. Succession plans, hopefully, are implemented only every twenty to thirty years or so. But the framework for succession, and the values, guidelines, and legalities needed, are prepared for well in advance of the need. It behooves families to sooner rather than later seek outside counsel, from their accountants, attorneys, board directors, and family business consultants. Their counsel is needed by the family to tackle the three types of succession every family business faces.

The three kinds of succession are: ownership succession, management succession, and contingency management succession in the event of an untimely death of an executive.

Complex **ownership succession** issues are beyond the scope of this book. Matters regarding gifting, estate plans, valuation and sale of the business, stock transfers, asset sales, insurance, revocable and irrevocable trusts, and divorce settlements require the expertise of accountants, attorneys, creative insurance experts, and experienced financial planners.[1] These professionals have a sense of urgency about having ownership succession plans in place now. Their wise counsel needs to be heard at family meetings.

**Management succession** has been a theme running throughout this book, especially the theme of executive leadership that is professionally competent, regardless of surname. The goal has to be the success of the business in the long run. This of course includes at least annual performance evaluations of the current executive. Anyone in the top spot of a family business has to meet the business requirements, company's purpose, values, and goals, and the leadership tests required by the family. Owners also must be assured that the current executive is adequately grooming a successor, and should be judged accordingly. The family thus accepts responsibility to always provide excellent leadership to the business.

The topic of **contingency management succession** is seldom discussed, and most likely seldom planned. Life can be unpredictable and tragically unfair. A bolt out of the blue can destroy a family business, if not the family itself. Cars and planes crash. Life disrupting illnesses happen. Divorces impact many families. Destructive behavior can harm a family irreparably. To prepare for these possibilities, families must devise a contingency plan to provide for an orderly, legal, and financially sound transition in the wake of a tragedy. This needs to be done for the long term viability of the business. This is especially compelling for younger families whose members are not yet educated, trained, or experienced enough to step in where bigger shoes would be left empty. It places a premium on hiring and grooming capable, trusted nonfamily managers who can be vested with the family's full trust and authority to carry on.

Grim as this topic may be, contingency management succession planning cannot be ignored. It can be likened to a fire drill; here it could be called a "death drill." The current executive needs to put owners and key personnel through periodic drills to make sure more than one person, in the event of a tragedy . . .

- Knows key customers
- Knows the key employees
- Knows the combination to the safe
- Has check signing authority
- Has access to bank accounts
- Knows the codes to the computer files
- Knows where the backup computer disks are
- Has a working relationship with the family business accountant, attorney, insurance agent, and banker
- Has a working relationship with professionals and business persons who can serve as mentors

This "death drill" can help spell out a formal contingency management plan at a series of family meetings, the resulting plan helping everyone in the family sleep better. And should tragedy befall a family, the family's grief and adjustment would not be compounded by a crisis in the business as well. It is being taken care of according to the death drill plan.

## Crisis Management

No family business is immune from a possible business crisis. Crises hit businesses everyday. Buildings burn down. A major law suit is filed and fought at draining cost. Difficult government regulation get imposed. Products get recalled. A major customer is lost. Abrupt cancellations of major contracts happen. Key employees defect. Markets adversely change, whether by demographics, deregulation, or global competition. Severe economic downturns or sharp interest rate hikes hit extremely hard. New technology renders products unprofitable or obsolete. Family businesses sail the uncertain seas of business daily. When a crisis strikes, the business must be able to develop a smart crisis management plan quickly, lest the family panic as though the sky were falling.

Emergency meetings usually and unfortunately exclude family members, who are, after all, owners of the business in crisis. Their exclusion on the surface seems justified, since the crisis is not a family crisis, but a business crisis and, thus, a management matter. But all owners should be included very early in the process of addressing the crisis for several reasons. If the owners live in the community, and are associated by the community with the business, then the owners need to be an informed, unified front to outsiders, including the general and business press. The family's public response to the crisis, let alone its response to employees, needs to be developed at a family ownership meeting.

These emergency meetings are not a democratic process, with time consuming consensus building belabored. Final decision making rests with those possessing coolheaded expertise and experience. But these decision makers would benefit from having to explain to family members their understanding of the crisis and their proposed response. It would be good rehearsal, especially when they have to mobilize employees, or when they have to respond to the public. They would benefit from the questions, insights, and suggestions from those not on the firing line—sometimes "outsiders" can see the obvious, the whole picture, or have a creative approach not thought of by the firefighters. Once decisions are made, it is helpful for the decision makers to proceed, having the support and authorization of all family owners.

All family owners need to be included in crisis emergency meetings. Their cooperation, sacrifice, financial commitment, and extra effort may be required to see the crisis response through to its conclusion. They are, when all is said and done, owners with a lot at stake in a crisis. They deserve to be included, especially when they are informed owners who are experienced at working with each other at family meetings.

## MAKING SURE

The owners of a family business have an enormous responsibility. It is up to them to assure the long-term success of the business. It is only a thriving business that can provide what all stakeholders desire—opportunities, options, and rewards. The owners, therefore, must know their stuff about owning a business. And they should make sure that everyone is capable of providing informed ownership. It is thus very appropriate for family owners to assure this in two ways.

The first way is the use of an annual, written check test. It can be given at a family meeting. It would include questions about the purpose of the family, the purpose of the business, and the values that are to shape conduct. It would cover basic knowledge of the business: from the past year's results to next year's goals; from the financial condition of the enterprise to knowledge of the legal/tax/financial instruments in effect; from the performance measures of the executives to the morale of the employees. It would also include knowledge of the succession plans, both normal and contingency plans.

The second method to make sure all owners are effective is the use of written performance feedback for each owner. Each owner would do a self-evaluation and an evaluation of the others, including parents. This annual review would provide useful, helpful feedback on how each contributed to the good of all and how each carried out his or her responsibilities and tasks over the year. It would provide feedback on how each owner lived up to the family's and company's values. And it would provide feedback on each person's progress in communicating effectively and cooperating fully.

This feedback could be handled on an individual, private basis, or it could be done openly at the family meeting—a meeting preferably facilitated by someone with expertise in performance feedback.

Too much to ask? Not really. The stakes are too high and the upside too promising not to make sure that everyone is meeting their obligations and living the values. A family business has to make sure its owners are effective.

## SUMMARY

Family meetings can be one of the best things a family owning a business can do. Collectively, the meeting of minds and hearts can yield results far greater than any one family member, or faction of the family, can produce alone.

The meetings need to be governed by mutually agreed upon rules, including communication rules, and facilitated by a competent meeting conductor.

The meetings should include all owners, and when appropriate, future family owners. Inviting trusted outside professionals should be considered.

The meetings should focus on ownership issues, not day-to-day operational, or management issues.

Family meetings can either unite a family to go forward with the business, for all the right reasons, or they can unite a family to not go forward, for all the right reasons.

Fundamentally, family meetings can help a family learn to respect and act on the necessary boundary between the family and its business—family is family, and business is business.

## BACK TO THE BASICS

1.  Take an informal survey of all your family business owners, asking them what they would like to understand better about the business.
2.  Also poll your owners about what rules for your family meetings are needed were you to have family meetings.
3.  How have you made it clear that ownership and management are not the same?
4.  Ask all your family business owners their understanding of your company's ownership succession plan.
5.  Also ask their understanding of the management succession plan.
6.  Conduct at least annual "death drills," so owners and key personnel can transition the business in an orderly fashion in the event of a tragedy to the current top executive.

## CHAPTER FOURTEEN

# What Good Is a Board of Directors?

*Years ago when we incorporated, our accountant and lawyer said that we had to have a board of directors. We didn't think much of it. Since I was in the front office I became the chairman, my brother was head of operations out in the shop so he became a director, his wife was our bookkeeper so she was on the board. And we asked our uncle, my dad's kid brother, to be on the board too. He's been with us forever and is our link to the past. So we thought, "What the hell, we got a board, nothing to it." Well, I'll tell you, that was some lazy thinking. When things got a lot more demanding and exacting in the auto industry, we got squeezed real bad. As a vendor we had to do exactly what the big boys demanded, at their price, or we were out of business. So things got tough around here. I started blaming my brother about what was going on in the shop. That made things rough in the office with his wife. They blamed me for bad leadership. Things were said that were better left unsaid. But they caused my brother to show up one day demanding me to sell out to him, or split the company in half— with him taking over the most profitable part. We contacted our lawyer. He said anything official had to be a board action. We had a board of directors meeting all right. It got real ugly. I felt sorry for our uncle. He doesn't say much, but you could tell he was hurt.*

*So now each side has a lawyer, we're threatening to sue each other, everything's at a standstill, and Thanksgiving is out for the first time ever. Our parents would be ashamed of us. So if you ask me, having a board of directors isn't worth much. At least not like we did it.*

Gerald, age 62, president/chairman
auto parts manufacturing

AN EFFECTIVE BOARD OF DIRECTORS CAN BE A VERY valuable family business tool. Families choosing to add directors to their leadership team are looking for help because they appreciate the high-wire act, with no net, that their businesses have become. This is not their fathers' business world.

Increasingly, family businesses are saying "the more help, the better." The more smart minds around the table, the better. The more experience from outside to speed up learning, the better. The more savvy, to give a competitive edge, the better. The more coaching, to see how good leadership really can become, the better. The more accountability, to promote improvement, focus, follow-up and follow-through, the better. The more level-headed wisdom, to lend confidence and comfort to all family members, the better. Family businesses are showing more enthusiasm for establishing boards of directors than at any time in history.

There had been a reluctance over the years, and in many cases a flat-out unwillingness, to have a board of directors with independent, outside members. Some families were embarrassed by how poorly they were doing, by how little money they were making, by how much indebtedness they were carrying, and by how much turmoil existed within their families and/or companies. Other families were resistant to adding independent, outside directors because they wanted no one, besides their accountants and bankers, to know how wealthy they were. And many mistakenly assumed that they would have to give up some of their ownership to outside directors—"Who would want to be on our board if they did not want to own part of our company?"

The new enthusiasm for setting up a board of directors with outside, independent directors has been aided by the good news that there are many highly qualified outsiders who would be honored to be asked to serve on a family-owned business board without any expectation whatsoever of acquiring some portion of ownership. These well-intended experts simply enjoy the opportunity to make a difference, to lend their knowledge and experience to help out, and to make a lasting contribution to a hardworking family that needs them. The psychological ownership they receive from making meaningful contributions outweighs equity ownership. The many professional business people willing to help family businesses are a tremendous resource. And they have either gone through the ups and downs of business themselves, or have seen it all, so they are unfazed by the troubles or wealth of the families that ask for their help.

## COMMON TIME TO SET UP A BOARD

Usually family businesses set up boards of directors toward the end of the founder's career. By this time the business has grown beyond the founder's energy and reach. The organization has gotten too complicated to run solo. Successors, ready or not, stand in the wings waiting to take over. The number of actual and future family owners has multiplied, including adult children, their spouses, their children and their grandchildren, making for a family of in-laws, step-children, cousins, grandchildren, and great grandchildren that the founder can hardly keep track of. Complicated financial instruments, like trusts and estates, have been set up. What were once $10,000 decisions have become multimillion dollar decisions with far-reaching impact. Opportunities to change the status quo are frequent: accept or reject the lucrative offers of competitors to buy the business; divide the business or spin off autonomous ventures for each child to run; take on debt to expand, to innovate, to remodel and overhaul, or to just keep up; sell part or all of the company to employees by forming an Employee Stock Ownership Plan (an ESOP); take the company public through an Initial Public Offering (an IPO); provide capital to children who want to strike out on their own; purchase back ownership shares of children who want to cash out. All these factors come into play during "the adolescence stage" of the corporate life cycle.[1] It is the time "when the company is too big for the old man to handle on his own, and the kids figure they can do a better job than he can anyway."

The founder, perhaps for the first time in his life, admits to himself and outloud that he cannot do it alone and that he needs help. He wants help for himself, for his children, and for his "baby" (the company). He wants a leadership team to back up his son or daughter who are in the driver's seat; a leadership team that is broader, more objective, and more experienced than he has available inside the company. He wants what he built for his family to be in as many good hands as possible after he dies. An effective and independent board of directors is looked to for just such help.

## INEFFECTIVE BOARDS OF DIRECTORS

One of the last things a family business needs is an ineffective board of directors. All boards are not created equal.

I have never seen an effective board made up solely of family members. A board of family members *only* can too easily be self-serving, with the long-range view seldom kept in focus. Objectivity, so needed on the leadership team, is not possible. Experience from elsewhere, let alone expertise in areas the family lacks, is not an influence. Family-only boards too easily can become internal surveillance committees when disagreements become cause for distrust. And selection of successors to key executive positions can too easily be simplistic: the divine right of the oldest, of the firstborn male, of the most aggressive, of the most winsome, rather than a selection based on the match between the company's strategic objectives and the skills, character and prior successes of the ideal candidate. The stakes are too high for a board that is at home around the kitchen table.

A board of directors cannot be effective when it is made up of actual or hoped-for allies of different family members. The founder should not try to stack the board with his or her "cronies" as the children likely would see their parents' selections of old friends and confidants. The second generation should not try to stack the board with only their contemporaries, hoping to marshal support for their interests only. One part of the family with more "connections" should not try to be overrepresented. The president of the family business should not try to hand pick directors that he or she is counting on to side with management. Boards made up of allies too easily become cozy, good ol' boy (or young boy, or gal) committees of passive, too narrowly focused, rubber-stamping yes-men— exactly what a family business least needs.

A family business also does not need the ineffective boards of yesterday that supposedly governed publicly traded companies. The traditional approach dutifully observed a wall between the board and management. Monday through Friday were the province of management; quarterly or biannual reports were the province of the board. Directors directed very little. They only interacted in person with the few executives who paraded before the board with overhead projector reports. Any director talking with employees or customers was seen as going behind the back of the president and his senior management team. Directors' decisions were based on voluminous board packets received by overnight delivery a day or two before the board meeting, making for fitful airplane reading en route to the meeting. Board meetings were cut-and-dried affairs, with banal questioning and unanimously approved motions the rule. Senior management, especially the president, saw directors as their followers at best, or someone to schmooze and get around at worst.

Then came the sea change in business over the past couple of decades. Fortune 500-sized companies were on their heels, if not on their backsides. Senior management was seen as mired in old ways. And boards were seen as sleeping at the switch. In some cases large institutional investors, such as pension funds, put the onus of responsibility directly on boards of directors. To their credit, many boards freed their directors to exercise the business skills and experience they brought to the boardroom table in the first place. The era of activist boards began.

Activist boards today go well beyond passive oversight. They are part of the company's leadership team, lending expertise and guidance to their companies. Directors are part of the team for setting direction and goals, strategic planning, reorganization, generating more business, investing in new technologies. Directors actively participate in evaluations involving company performance and the chief executive. They are demanding accountability of senior management, particularly the top person. And they can be the eyes and ears of the company. Home Depot of Atlanta goes so far as to require its directors to make between eight and ten unannounced store visits each quarter to anonymously interview customers and openly interview employees. The home improvement chain thus learns, from directors no less, about dirty floors, congested parking lots, customer satisfaction, employee needs, and companywide communication. Home Depot's aim is to be helped by directors who know and understand the business they are directing.[2] Other companies insist that their directors attend their industry trade shows where they can meet customers and suppliers, observe competitors, observe company personnel in action, and learn industry trends.

Huge companies and small family businesses alike cannot suffer ineffective, irrelevant boards of directors gladly or any longer. All companies need the help that effective, activist boards can provide.

## WHAT AN EFFECTIVE BOARD CAN DO

An effective board of directors has one job: help the company succeed over the long term. Small, privately held companies, which most family businesses are, especially need all the help they can get. The board's sole duty is to serve all owners of the business—family members, future family members, partners. The board's first responsibility is thus to owners, collaborating especially with company executives and the company's accountants, attorneys, and bankers, all working as a leadership team on business matters to assure long-term success. It is the company's long-term success, after all, that the family benefits from the most.

At a minimum, an effective board can help a family business in the following ways:

1. Help the company define why it exists and what needs it fulfills; in other words, help the company make explicit its purpose and mission.
2. Help set company direction for the next ten years, the next five years, the next year.
3. Help with succession planning, grooming and selection of the next executives, assuring the company will successfully transition to new leadership in the event of an untimely death, or to the next generation when the time has come.
4. Help establish realistic, sound objectives that when fulfilled will take the company in the decided direction.
5. Help set clear goals with strategies that will meet the goals. Included here is helping put a budget in place that includes capital investments, whether new equipment or buildings.
6. Help set up a process to review measurements, from financial scorekeeping to customer surveys, from employee input to market share, from timelines to performance reviews of key personnel, so the family knows how things are going. These reviews need to be at regularly set intervals, some monthly, like the second Wednesday of the month at 2:00 P.M., others quarterly or semiannually at specified times that are consistent year to year.
7. Help with decision making by assisting upper management
   • to think through complex issues from every angle
   • to analyze all possible options for solution
   • to guide the final selection of solutions
   • to set valid measurements and timelines
8. Help keep the company out of trouble by serving as a reality check to pie-in-the-sky projections; overly exuberant sales outlooks; expansions that cannot be supported by company resources, whether manpower, money, infrastructure, or time; unrealistic growth demands that would require ethical compromises by employees to meet the numbers or else.

9. Help sound the alert on changes in the marketplace and economy, or on emerging internal problems, obstacles, and needs.

10. Help manage through tough times, such as crises, business downturns, problems associated with inflation and deflation, cash flow difficulties, debt restructuring, cost-cutting needs.

11. Help serve as a catalyst to action when more of the same will not do, when complacency and satisfaction with past successes get in the way, when good enough isn't, when boldness is called for to exploit a solid opportunity.

12. Help select the financial instruments recommended by the company's accountant, attorney, and banker, from estate planning to workers' benefits, from financial controls to earnings distributions.

13. Help make decisions family members either do not want to make, or decisions best made by nonfamily members. One example would be executive compensation. A compensation committee of outside directors, as is required of publicly traded companies, could be established to set the president's and key managers' salaries and bonus structure, making sure both are aligned with company values, direction, goals, strategy, and results. Another example of a decision best left to outsiders: earnings distributions to shareholders that are in balance with company needs to reinvest, pay down debt, have cash reserves, or meet legal requirements.

14. Help mentor executive leadership in hopes he or she will absorb ten years of experience in two.

15. Help evaluate the performance of executive leadership, holding executives accountable with objective measurements and personal feedback.

16. Help provide contacts, introductions, and networking avenues so executive leadership has access to even more help.

17. Help generate new business by bringing in new customers and "talking up" the business in wider circles.

18. Help bring prestige to the company by directors lending their reputations to the family's business.

19. Exercise fiduciary responsibilities to owners by assuring management compliance with the law and the highest of business ethics. This includes making sure that the company's auditor is professionally independent and acceptable to all shareholders, owners, and partners.

## WHAT AN EFFECTIVE BOARD OF DIRECTORS LOOKS LIKE

Family members understandably do not want to lose control of their business to some outsiders, no matter how well-meaning and talented the outsiders are. No one wants to give up the "baby" for adoption. These families are more comfortable having more family members on their boards than outside, independent directors. Other families simply feel "the more help the better" is the way to go, so they either have an even balance of family to independent directors, or more independent directors. There is certainly no hard and fast rule. The guiding thought ought to be the needs of the business.

### Composition

Optimum size of a board is between five and nine members. Any less reduces creativity and needed balance; any more proves cumbersome, inefficient, and interpersonally too complicated.

Family businesses also benefit from diversity on their boards. It is a good idea to have both men and women on the board, a very rare practice in corporate America. Some family members may relate much more easily to a particular gender, and in family businesses *family* matters. It is good to have directors from two generations—gray hair is good, peak of career is good. It is best to have differing expertise on the board: someone from the industry the family's business is in; someone with financial and/or legal background; someone experienced in family business; someone with a marketing background, a manufacturing background, an international business background—whatever expertise is needed to have a well balanced board.

It is also a good practice to have a family member serve as chairperson of the board. Commonly this would be the founder, or a family member who is not the president or chief executive officer. The family chairperson may not be as experienced with boardsmanship as some of the outsiders, but family comfort and sense of ownership are important. Informal leadership among board members inevitably develops anyway. I have, however, worked for a family business over a two-year period that has an outsider as its board chair. The family itself is simply too young and too small to provide board leadership. This arrangement has proved more than satisfactory, since the chairperson is trustworthy, respected, and skilled at bringing people together. His motivation for everyone succeeding is readily apparent to all. Having an independent, outside chairperson also makes good sense when two or more family entities have equal ownership.

## Selection

Selection of board members is a crucially important task. It is an ownership responsibility. Family members, sitting informally at a family owners' meeting, or representatives from the family, when the family is large and several generations are of age, sitting formally as a Family Council, have the say about qualifications, recruitment, and final selection of directors.

Qualifications of family directors are of course less stringent than for independent outside directors. With two-to-three-year overlapping terms, all family members eventually can rotate membership on the board. It is the most egalitarian way to practice fairness within the family.

Qualifications of outside, independent directors are another matter. The family deserves the best, the brightest, the most experienced, the most distinguished, the most helpful persons they can find. Family members need to look for outside directors . . .

- Who enjoy helping others grow and succeed
- Who have succeeded in their own right
- Who possess expertise in areas the family needs
- Who have the time
- Who have a generalist's view of the big picture over the long haul

- Who are effective listeners and straight talkers
- Who have a feel and empathy for family relationships
- Who appreciate the value and benefit of differing opinions
- Who have a feel, if not in-depth experience, for the industry the family business is in
- Who know what effective leadership does and understand how to further develop it
- Who know what organizational effectiveness is and understand how to further develop it
- Who are financially literate
- Who will ask all the "dumb" questions that need to be asked, like "why are we doing this?," "what are the customers saying?," "what are we assuming here?"
- Who will ask all the tough questions that need to be asked, like "why weren't our agreed upon goals met?," "why after so much fanfare in the beginning wasn't this followed through?," "why weren't they kept informed?," "is this fair?," "do we really want to saddle the next generation with this obligation?"
- Who are skilled at giving feedback, both positive and constructively critical, to anyone in the family and company
- Who believe in accountability as a tool to help people become more successful
- Who will not be too chummy with family members and senior management, or too aloof—objectivity and independent thinking balanced by empathy are what is needed
- Who are always motivated by the question, "What is right and best for the family owners?"

## Recruitment

Once family members establish directors' qualifications, they will need to begin a search. They can ask successful business and professional people they know for candidates. They can contact their trade associations for names. Once a good list is developed and potential directors are called to ascertain their interest, the family needs to send them a copy of the purpose of the business, the family/company values, a brief history of the business, and marketing materials the company uses. Along with this material is a copy of desired qualifications of board directors, presented in the form of a questionnaire. Candidates are requested to explain their fit with the company, and to provide references which are pursued by the family.

The most likely candidates are invited to a series of one-on-one interviews with family members, especially with the founder and the present senior executive, and group interviews with other family members. A tour of the company, preferably conducted by a nonfamily employee, and including an informal meeting with a handful of employees from across the company, would be invaluable. Candidates would also be encouraged to consult with the family's accountant, attorney, banker, and family business consultant to learn more about the kind of help needed.

Additionally, director candidates should be told the length of their term on the board, usually one or two terms of two or three years—long enough to make meaningful contributions, short enough to prevent burnout.

Directors' compensation should also be discussed. Paying all of a director's expenses to attend board meetings is a given, including travel, lodging, meals, and entertainment. Regarding director fees, however, it is often best to ask candidates what they consider fair compensation. Some will have a daily or meeting fee. Some may simply want to be included in the company's medical insurance program. Some may wish free use of the company's products or services. Whatever is decided, the family should remember two things: with the exception of someone very charitable who will serve freely, "you get what you pay for"; and directors' fees are investments, not overhead.

## Liability

Before a candidate consents to join the board, the family needs to pass along the counsel of its attorney regarding the legal liabilities of being a director. Counsel's advice is also shared about the advisability of having indemnification, such as directors' and officers' (D & O) insurance. Research has shown, however, that litigation against privately held companies is rare, a far less threat than generally perceived.[3] And some states, like Wisconsin and Texas, have strong legislative protections for directors.[4] Some private companies choose to have advisory boards rather than formal boards of directors. They do this in part to retain full authority over their companies, taking the advisors' input into merely casual consideration. But they also choose advisory boards in hopes of dodging liability issues. Legal decisions, however, have rendered the distinction between advisory boards and boards of directors meaningless: "a rose by any other name is still a rose, because [advisors] typically are doing everything they otherwise would do as a director."[5] Bottom line, families and their directors obviously need to follow legal counsel on this directors' legal liability issue.

## Orientation

Once directors are selected, a thorough orientation is a must. New directors need to interview all family members to learn their hopes, dreams and desires for and from the business. They need to interview both key personnel and a cross section of employees to ascertain organizational strengths and needs. Directors should be given all key documents and financial data, as well as explanations of financial instruments in place for the owners. Several lengthy individual interviews should take place again with the founder and the president. New directors also ought to meet fellow board members. Having a casual dinner with each director would go a long way to establishing board chemistry. Directors simply cannot help lead a company if they are not solidly "in the know," and if they do not have working relationships at least started before their first meeting.

## Retreat

When a family first establishes a board, or when new directors come on board, it is a good practice for the family, or representatives of the family on the Family Council, the senior management team, and the board to get away together for a couple days. The first order of business has to be answers to questions such as:

- What is the purpose of the board?
- What is its role?
- What are its top three responsibilities?

- What is its authority?
- Who is authorized to speak on behalf of the board?
- What is expected before, during, and in between meetings?
- What are the guidelines of conduct?
- What are the confidentiality and nondisclosure requirements?
- How best can it be of most help to the family?
- How best can it be of most help to the president?

## Leadership-Team Best Practices

Another crucial topic for the orientation or annual retreat is discussion of leadership-team best practices. No leadership team can function very successfully without its members interacting with each other on the basis of

*Mutual trust*: everyone needs to be able to count on each other, everyone's word is good, everyone is seen pulling together for the good of all

*Mutual respect*: everyone needs to value what everyone brings to the table

*Mutual understanding*: how many meetings in the parking lot or on the phone are needed to understand what just took place?— better to take a few minutes after each issue or decision to make sure everyone is on the same page

*Mutual support*: the opposites of mutual support are failing to back each other up, leaving someone to "hang out there high and dry," not giving each other a hand, not offering help early enough

*Mutual accountability*: everyone receives credit when credit is due, everyone's feet are held to the fire when commitments are not kept, everyone receives performance feedback for recognition and improvement

*Team unity*: a leadership team needs to foster differences of opinion and encourage vigorous debate for the sake of higher quality decision making; but once decisions are made, no matter how heated things get behind the scenes, the board presents a unified front to the world, mindful that "a house divided against itself cannot stand."

All of these necessary behaviors between members of the leadership team are mutually interdependent. Missing one, the rest are compromised. Like a wagon wheel, if one spoke breaks down, the whole wagon either wobbles dangerously or crashes. Discussions at the kickoff retreat need to include everyone's views on what it takes for each person present to practice these leadership team behaviors.

## LEADERSHIP-TEAM BEST PRACTICES

## Meetings

Regarding frequency of board meetings, need takes precedence over formula. If the board is newly constituted, or the company is going through hell and high water, the board of directors might need to meet several days in one week, or several times in one month. When things are going along smoothly, bimonthly or quarterly meetings are appropriate. When the board enjoys good chemistry and has a good working relationship with the senior management team, and nothing is pressing, meetings can be conducted on conference calls, with face-to-face meetings occurring biannually. One of these should be an extended meeting dedicated to annual performance review and setting direction, goals, and strategies for the next year.

## Between Meetings

Directors should receive calls on a monthly basis at least from the company's president to pass along information and keep communication channels open. Directors should be free to contact the president as well. And since this is a family business, and the directors serve the whole family, ongoing dialogue between directors and family members should not be ruled out. Openness about these conversations will prevent actual or perceived coalitions. All directors should be asked at least twenty days before board meetings for any special topics they want placed on the agenda—a board meeting agenda is not the sole province of executive management. Directors should receive board packets at least ten working days prior to meetings, so time at meetings is not wasted on information gathering. Directors are thus spared the expectation to be brilliant off the cuff. Furthermore, it should be required that the minutes of each meeting be sent to each director within the first week following the meeting.


## THE BOARD AND THE PRESIDENT

One of the best things a board of directors can do for a family business is help its president, whether the president is an old pro or new on the job, whether family member or outsider, whether selected with help from the board or selected by the founder. Helping the president, however, is easier said than done.

Across the corporate landscape are stories of poor relations between executives and directors. Directors are accused of arrogance, acting as though they know it all; of micromanaging the company's details; of going behind the backs of executives; of giving uninformed, or biased, or outdated advice; of not understanding the business or its industry; of being irrelevant because they drop in for a day or two a few times a year, enjoy a convivial dinner or the resort amenities, and then go home: "That's called directing a company?"

Directors accuse executives of jealously protecting their turf, not wanting help, being arrogant about what is right for the company, being headstrong about doing what he or she darn well pleases, not wanting performance feedback, keeping directors in the dark, feeding them what they want to hear, or feeding them what the executive wants them to hear.

These tensions are normal and inevitable when a group of leaders gets together. There are no followers. It is like trying to herd cats. Given there is no way to avoid board/executive stress, it is important, nonetheless, to minimize the intensity or degree of tension. Concerted efforts must be made to create constructive working relationships.

One thing directors can do is make it abundantly and repeatedly clear to the president what their motives are. They want to help. They want to make a difference. They want the president to succeed. They do not want to hinder, get in the way, have their way, or subtract from anything. They want to add. Motivations like these must be conveyed to the president by each director informally, and they must be echoed formally at board meetings. Actions to prove them are more likely given these public commitments.

Another thing directors can do is to invite the president to select one of them, or an outsider who would report to the board, to serve the president as coach, mentor, confidant, sounding board, paid friend, or whatever name would be most palatable to the president.

This coach should meet regularly with the president, spending 75 percent of the time listening, 25 percent of the time asking how he or she can help. How else can mutual trust and mutual respect and mutual support develop?

The outside directors can also invite the president to select one or two directors as liaisons to the rest of the family not represented on the board. Since it is family matters that usually are the most difficult in family businesses, the directors could establish bridges of understanding between the family and its company's president. Things can be said and straightened out more easily more times than not when done in private with a mediating outsider. The president would benefit from the good offices provided by some of the directors.

Presidents, on the other hand, can reduce the common frictions between themselves and directors as well. They can appreciate how "the more help, the better" approach is the way to go. They can appreciate that it is smart sometimes to abandon themselves to the ideas of others. They can keep directors more informed than the directors themselves even want. They can regularly call directors to keep communications open. They can return directors' calls the same day received. They can ask directors about their experiences. They can ask directors what they would do if they were sitting at the desk where the buck stops. They can ask directors to teach something of their expertise or special interest at future board meetings or to employees. They can invite a director or two to join them on visits to customers and benchmarked companies, as well as to accompany them to trade association meetings or trade shows. And they can ask directors informally for feedback, giving directors an opening to both compliment and reinforce good performance, something few executives ever receive, and to suggest how things could be improved. These efforts by both directors and family business presidents are all in service of one thing—doing what is best for the entire family over the long run. No president or director is above this responsibility.

## PERFORMANCE FEEDBACK

Mutual accountability is a value, and as such it is an important tool to bring out the best in people. This tool can be at least partially exercised by the use of performance feedback for both the company's president and for the directors. Each deserves performance feedback to reinforce the good and improve the not-so-good.

### Feedback for the President

It has been implied above that it is good practice for directors to be giving informal performance feedback to the president all along the way. It is equally good for the president to be inviting informal feedback all along the way as well. There should be no surprises!

It is, however, valuable for the directors on an annual basis to give more formal and complete feedback to the president. A performance-feedback questionnaire can be created by the directors and the president. It would be filled out by each director, the president using it as self-assessment, and by family members chosen by the president and the board, if not all of them. The content of the complete feedback, which would include the questionnaire responses, should focus on . . .

- Year-end company performance data
- Surveys from customers
- Surveys of employee morale and organizational health
- Measurements of goals fulfilled
- Opinions about the president's strengths and weaknesses
- The president's communication skills
- Perceptions of the president role modeling the family's and the company's values
- Efforts to groom an appropriate successor, regardless of the age of the president
- Continuing education and personal-improvement efforts

- Reports from the liaison directors about the president's relations with family members
- Reports from the executive coach
- Bonuses for the past year, based on all of the above, and compensation levels for the year ahead

The outside director who is the president's coach, or an outside director working with the hired coach, should be the person to compile the above information and present it to the president privately a week or so prior to the annual board meeting. It is best for this feedback to be dialogue, not a one-way lecture or sermon. The entire board also receives the feedback report and has a week to think it over prior to the meeting. At the annual meeting the president's performance feedback should be the first item on the agenda, to get it over with! It should not last longer than an hour, and preferably should be focused on goals and expectations for the next year.

## Feedback for the Directors

Mutual accountability means feedback to directors as well. This is a joint responsibility of family members, or their representatives, and the president of the company. Together they can create a directors' feedback questionnaire that is to be filled out by family members, the president, fellow directors, and each director using the form as a self-assessment.

The content of this annual feedback should include the following:

- How well the director understands the family's desires
- How well the director understands the business and its industry
- How well the director contributes to the direction and strategic planning of the company
- How well prepared the director has been for meetings
- How well the director listens, talks straight, and speaks up
- How well the director maintains objectivity
- How well the director focuses on the long term
- How well the director relates to all family members, to the president, to senior management, and to fellow directors

- How available and responsive the director has been to lend expertise when needed
- How the director contributes to good board chemistry
- How creative and innovative the director has been
- How the director seeks to bring out the best in the president

The chairperson of the board should compile the questionnaire results and meet with each director separately and privately prior to the annual meeting. An hour should be set aside at the annual meeting immediately following the president's feedback for general discussion of board performance. Improvement goals for the next year can be set.

These performance feedback exercises are an invaluable tool for family businesses whose owners' approach to family life and business life begins and ends with, "I want you to succeed, I want to succeed, I want all of us to succeed, I want the business to succeed beyond all of our lives."

## SUMMARY

It is common sense that a family business should not try to go it alone in the demanding and ruthlessly competitive business world we all work in. An excellent family business tool is a board of directors. A board of directors can help the family and its business navigate successfully into the future.

An effective board of directors includes family members and outside, independent experts chosen by the family. These outsiders do not gain any ownership of the business. They do, however, gain satisfaction from making a difference in the life of a family-owned business. This psychological ownership is augmented by mutually agreed upon fees.

The board is part of the company's leadership team, helping direct the company from the perspective of big picture, long range success. The board assists the company's senior management team, especially its president, by lending needed expertise, experience, guidance, and oversight.

The effectiveness of the board's help is measured by the progress of the company, the growth of its leadership, and the rewards enjoyed by the family today and tomorrow.

## BACK TO THE BASICS

1. Hold a family owners meeting to discuss what additional help and expertise the family and its business needs to assure long-term success.

2. Ask family owners, company leaders, and employees to explain the company's long-term direction, current goals and strategy plans, financial instruments in place, and measurement of results. If the answers betray lack of accuracy and clarity, confusion, and "we don't have any," it is time to set up a board of directors.

3. Interview business people, as well as the company's accountant, attorney, banker, and family business consultant, for their experiences with boards of directors. Learn what is and is not helpful.

4. List five concrete ways your family business is developing its current and future leadership. Can you conclude you are doing a good job?

5. If you already have a board of directors in place, engage your directors and senior management team in a discussion of how well the board is executing the nineteen jobs of an effective board listed above.

# Fifty-five Best Practices of Family Business

## 1

Give top priority to both family and business (chap. 1).

## 2

Respect the boundary between family life and business life (chap. 1).

## 3

Respect the boundary between ownership and management (chap. 1).

## 4

Treat the family's business as a responsibility, not a privilege (chap. 2).

# 5

Make sure the family's business has
effective leadership (chap. 3).

# 6

Spell out a sense of purpose for the
family business (chap. 3).

# 7

Practice personal values at work
(chap. 3).

# 8

Focus every activity in the family's business
on satisfying the customer (chap. 3).

# 9

Treat employees as responsible partners
(chap. 3).

# 10

Use a merit-based reward system for all
employees (chap. 3).

# 11

Parents: share with your children
your love and passion for the
business (chap. 4).


# 12

Parents: make clear to your children the
requirements of employment
in the family's
business (chaps. 4 and 13).


# 13

Parents: insist your children's work
experiences are reinforced by
feedback from coaches,
mentors, employees, and
family members (chap. 4).


# 14

Parents: keep current with
the world of business
throughout your
careers (chap. 4).


# 15

Parents: gradually let go of control as
your business and children
mature (chap. 4).

# 16

Keep family members whose
personalities clash from
working with each
other (chap. 4).

# 17

Make sure everyone is focused
on big business
goals (chap. 4).

# 18

Make sure family issues are
left outside the door of
the company (chap. 4).

# 19

Treat family members at work as
though they were nonfamily
employees (chap. 4).

# 20

Praise family members publicly for
good work (chap. 4).

# 21

Correct family members privately
regarding mistakes, poor
performance, or poor
behavior (chap. 4).

# 22

Deal directly with family members,
rather than talking behind
their backs to third
parties (chap. 4).

# 23

Appreciate family members' capacity
to think before offering
them advice (chap. 4).

# 24

Appreciate the good intentions
behind unsolicited
advice (chap. 4).

# 25

Use persuasion, rather than orders, to get
things done with family
members (chap. 4).

## 26

Parents: give equal attention
to all children working in the
company (chap. 4).

## 27

Children: show parents and
grandparents gratitude for the
opportunities that you
have been given (chap. 4).

## 28

Choose to be close to family members at
work, rather than being right, with
some exceptions (chap. 4).

## 29

Couples: choose friendship as
the foundation of your
marriage (chap. 6).

## 30

Couples: practice mutual trust and
mutual respect as the way to
strengthen your friendship
with each other (chap. 6).

# 31

Couples: achieve a friendly parting from
your parents in order to be
a grown-up couple in your
own right (chap. 6).

# 32

Couples: make time for
pleasurable activities with each
other (chap. 6)

# 33

Couples: appreciate each other's
differences, rather than trying to change
each other (chap. 6).

# 34

Couples: care for each other equally,
rather than having a care giver/child
relationship (chap. 6).

# 35

Couples: keep in mind that being flexible
with each other, rather than rigid,
paves the way to closeness
and growth (chap. 6).

## 36

Parents: make the time to enjoy your
children and grandchildren (chap. 7).

## 37

Parents: tell your children important and
amusing family stories, along with
stories about the family's
business (chaps. 7 and 13).

## 38

Parents: always be alert to minimize
sibling rivalry between the
children (chap. 7).

## 39

Parents: forge the only healthy coalition
in a family—the one between
yourselves (chap. 7).

## 40

Parents: nurture your children's natural
desire to become grown-ups in
their own right (chap. 7).

# 41

Adult children: motivated by gratitude,
find mature ways to honor your
parents (chap. 8).

# 42

Parents: give your children
permission, all through
their lives, to succeed (chap. 9).

# 43

Family members: understand and resolve
your own grief, and help others with
theirs, after suffering a loss due
to death or divorce (chap. 10).

# 44

Families: seek medical intervention
for loved ones showing signs of
Alzheimer's disease (chap. 10).

# 45

Families: make explicit your personal
and business values to guide everyone's
business behavior (chap. 11).

# 46

Families: adopt positive communication
beliefs to motivate others to meet
the communication needs of
the company (chap. 12).

# 47

Families: train everyone in your family
and in your business in the arts of careful
listening and straight talk (chap. 12).

# 48

Families: hold informal meetings to keep
everyone involved, informed, and
contributing (chap. 13).

# 49

Families: hold formal meetings to address
ownership issues that will help all family
members  become good owners (chap. 13).

# 50

Large families and those into the third
generation: create a family council to
formally carry out ownership
responsibilities (chap. 13).

# 51

Families: adopt rules to effectively guide
family meetings (chap. 13).

# 52

Families: hire an outside facilitator to
effectively manage emotional and
controversial issues that need to be
addressed at family meetings (chap. 13).

# 53

Families: make sure all owners of the
business are knowledgeable and
responsible owners by using
written check tests for knowledge
and written performance feedback
for responsibilities (chap. 13).

# 54

A board of directors that includes
outside experts can be an invaluable
tool for further success (chap. 14).

# 55

Family owners, the executive leadership
in their company, and their board of
directors: practice mutual
accountability (chap. 14).

# NOTES

**Introduction**

1. Mike Cohn, *Passing the Torch*, 2d ed. (New York: McGraw-Hill, 1992), 10.

**Chapter 1**

1. Joan Magretta, "Governing the Family-Owned Enterprise: An Interview with Finland's Krister Ahlstrom," *Harvard Business Review*, January–February 1998, 112.

**Chapter 2**

1. Peter Drucker, *Managing in a Great Time of Change* (Dalton, N.Y.: Truman Tally Books/Dutton, 1995), 57.

**Chapter 3**

1. Max DePree, *Leadership Is an Art* (New York: Doubleday, 1989); *Leadership Jazz* (New York: Dell, 1992).

2. James Collins and Jerry Porras, *Built To Last* (New York: Harper Business, 1994), 46.

**Chapter 4**
1. Charles Fishman, "The War for Talent," *Fast Company*, August 1998, 106.

**Chapter 5**
1. MPL Communications Ltd./Faber Music, London, 1990.

**Chapter 7**
1. Genesis 4:1–15; 27; 37; Luke 15:11–32.
2. Salvador Minuchin, *Families and Family Therapy* (Cambridge: Harvard University Press, 1974).
3. Jay Haley, *Leaving Home* (New York: McGraw-Hill, 1980).

**Chapter 8**
1. Exodus 20:12.
2. Ernest Thompson, screenplay, *On Golden Pond*, directed by Mark Rydell, Director, Live Entertainment/ITC, 1981.

**Chapter 9**
1. Isaiah 2:17, Romans 12:3, Titus 6:10, Luke 18:18-30, Luke 12:13-21, Mark 12:42–44, Mark 10:25.

**Chapter 10**
I have relied professionally over the years, and in this chapter, upon the thoughtful, well researched work of William Worden. Although written for the helping professions, his book has deserved a wider audience.

1. William J. Worden, *Grief Counseling and Grief Therapy* (New York: Springer Publishing, 1982), 11–16.
2. Ibid., 17.
3. Ibid., 16.
4. Ibid., 19–33.
5. Alzheimer's Association, 1919 North Michigan Ave., Chicago, IL, 60611-1676, 1-800-272-3900.

## Chapter 11

1. Anne Remley, "From Obedience to Independence," *Psychology Today*, October 1988, 56.

2. Patrick Kelley, President/CEO of Physicians Sales and Services, in a speech to the National Committee of Employee Ownership national conference in Chicago, April, 1995.

3. James Collins and Jerry Porras, "Building Your Company's Vision," *Harvard Business Review*, September–October 1996, 67–68.

4. John S. McCollum, "Good Enough?" *Industry Week*, 20 February 1995.

5. Kelly, op cit.

## Chapter 12

1. Thomas Gordon, *Parent Effectiveness Training* (New York: Peter H. Wyden, 1970), 29-138.

## Chapter 13

1. Cohn, op cit, p. 119 ff.

## Chapter 14

1. Ichak Adizes, *Corporate Lifecycles: How and Why Corporations Grow and Die and What to Do About It* (Englewood Cliffs, N.J.: Prentice Hall, 1988), 45.

2. Lublin, Joann, "Corporate Chiefs Polish Their Relations with Directors," *Wall Street Journal*, 15 October 1993.

3. John L. Ward. *Creating Effective Boards for Private Enterprises* (San Francisco: Jossey-Bass Publishers, 1996), 78.

4. Dale D. Buss, "How Advisers Can Help You Grow," *Nation's Business*, March 1996, 50.

5. Ibid., 50.

# RECOMMENDED READING

## BUSINESS MATTERS

Adizes, Ichak. *Corporate Lifecycles*. Englewood Cliffs, N.J.: Prentice Hall, 1988.

Autry, James. *Love & Profit*. New York: William Morrow and Co., 1991.

Belasco, James, and Ralph Stayer. *Flight of the Buffalo*. New York: Warner Books, 1993.

Case, John. *Open-Book Management*. New York: Harper Business, 1994.

Cohn, Mike. *Passing the Torch*. 2d ed. New York: McGraw-Hill, 1992.

Collins, James, and Jerry Porras. *Built to Last*. New York: Harper Business, 1994.

DePree, Max. *Leadership Is An Art*, New York: Doubleday, 1989.

———. *Leadership Jazz*. New York: Dell, 1992.

Drucker, Peter. *Managing in a Time of Change*. New York: Truman Tally Books/Dutton, 1995.

Flannery, Thomas, David Hofrichter and Paul Platten. *People, Performance & Pay*. New York: The Free Press, 1996.

Kouzes, James, and Barry Posner. *Credibility*. San Francisco: Jossey-Bass, 1993.

Scott, Mary and Howard Rothman. *Companies With a Conscience*. New York: Citadel Press, 1992.

Stack, Jack. *The Great Game of Business*. New York: Doubleday Currency, 1992.


## FAMILY MATTERS


Bodenhammer, Gregory. *Parent in Control*. New York: Simon & Shuster, 1995.

Brazelton, T. Barry. *Touch Points*. Reading, Mass.: Addison-Wesley, 1992.

Briggs, Dorothy. *Your Child's Self-Esteem*. Garden City, N.Y.: Doubleday, 1975.

Dinkman, D., and G. Michael. *Parenting Teenagers*. American Guidance Service, Circle Pines, Minn., 55014-1796: 1990.

Faber, A., and E. Mazlish. *Siblings Without Rivalry*. New York: Avon Books, 1987.

Gannon, Margaret. *Gourmet Parenting*. 2d ed. LaCresta Foundation, 251 Panorama Drive, Bakersfield, CA, 93305, 1997.

Ginott, Haim. *Between Parent & Child*. New York: MacMillan Company, 1965.

Gordon, Thomas. *Parent Effective Training*, New York: Peter H. Wyden, 1970.

Guerney, Louise. *Parenting: A Skills Training Manual*, Ideals Inc., 11910 Renwood Lane, North Bethesda, MD, 20852, 1995.

Hendrix, Harville. *Getting the Love You Want*. New York: Henry Holt, 1988.

Nielson, J., and S. Glenn. *Positive Discipline*. New York: Ballantine, 1996.

Pittman, Frank. *Turning Points*. New York: W. W. Norton & Company, 1987.

# INDEX

# ABOUT THE AUTHOR

Neil N. Koenig, Ph.D., draws on thirty years of experience working with families in this exploration of what every family business should know. Having a master's degree in theology and a doctorate in clinical psychology, he has worked with families as a pastor and as a family psychologist. He taught behavioral sciences and trained physicians for family practice residency training programs of the University of California Schools of Medicine.

For the past twelve years Koenig has been consulting with both family and nonfamily businesses, focusing especially on leadership issues with executives and their leadership teams, including boards of directors.

Koenig is much sought after across the country as a conference speaker, family meeting facilitator, and management retreat facilitator.

Koenig regularly humbles himself as an experienced fly fisherman and a perfectly lousy golfer and skier.

He can be contacted at the following addresses:

Mailing address:

Neil N. Koenig
132 Cindy Avenue
Clovis, CA 93612

Web site address:

www.nkoenig.com

Phone addresses:

559.323.9355
559.323.1795 fax

email address:

nk@nkoenig.com